Mastering Business Administration in Education and African politics
(The Sierra Leone chapter)

Completed and compiled by

Mohamed Sannoh

BA (Commerce) University of Abertay Dundee, Scotland, PgC.BA (Education),
University of Keele, England

Formerly: Head of Business Management Department,
Methodist Boys' High School, Freetown-Sierra Leone (1994-1998)

Founder of the Institute of Commercial Management (ICM) education system in Sierra
Leone and The Gambia

Order this book online at www.trafford.com
or email orders@trafford.com

Most Trafford titles are also available at major online book retailers.

Printed in the United States of America.

ISBN: 978-1-4669-6558-4 (sc)
ISBN: 978-1-4669-6560-7 (hc)
ISBN: 978-1-4669-6559-1 (e)

Library of Congress Control Number: 2012920116

Trafford rev. 10/24/2012

 www.trafford.com

North America & international
toll-free: 1 888 232 4444 (USA & Canada)
phone: 250 383 6864 ♦ fax: 812 355 4082

**About the author:** Mohamed Sannoh loves teaching than politics. Teachers struggle to get their salaries, but still live longer and go to heaven when they die but the stupid and evil politicians enjoy more. They squander the nation's wealth to buy houses in Babylon. They send their children there to study whilst their nation's schools are left impoverished. When these politicians die, hell is their destination. *"What good is it for a man to gain the whole world, yet forfeit his soul?"* is a biblical question that Disciple Mark asked in verse 36 of Chapter 8 of his gospel but have any of these politicians ever had time to think over their "leadership?" Would you like to be a teacher to live longer and go to heaven or a politician to die earlier and go to hell? Judgment day has the answer!

For the ten years he gave to the profession, engaged in teaching Business Studies, preparing matured mixed ability students for the UK Institute of Commercial Management professional qualifications in his native Sierra Leone and neighbouring peaceful adopted second home, The Gambia, Mohamed Sannoh discovered that there is a dared need for continuous former education designed purposely for African politicians if only they mean business for the better and not the greedy.

"I am not impressed because all of our politicians of today and in the past except Sir Milton Margai, who retired earlier into Heaven, leaving Siaka Stevens in charge to teach corruption downwards to the least palm wine tapper in Binkolo" and handed over to Joseph Saidu Momoh who shamefully wrecked my country into civil war through economic mismanagement, womanising and drunkenness. These have all woefully failed; including the United Nation's Tejan Kabbah and **Ernest Bai Koroma,** a Christian but conjures "sokobana" at State house.

During Ernest's term of office under APC rule of recent, the nation's tribal statistics figures are politically falsified into shamefully revealing that the Temnes, sharing the North with the Limbas, Yalunkas, Sosos, Lokos, Korankos, etc. are now the largest population of the tribal groups. The speed of sale of national land to foreign western investors have alarmed the nation in many quarters that if Koroma stays in power for the second term, Sierra Leone will soon be heading into another Zimbabwe.

This has given cause to begin to consider the SLPP's Maada Bio for a full stop to future calamities that may involve our great grand children into the causes of driving foreign land grabbers out of our country. Upon completion of PTLLS recently at the College of North West London, Mohamed Sannoh returns to the Dundee Business School, University of Abertay Dundee in Scotland to read more and more and more; at the time of going to press. Have you got problem with that?

About the book: The purpose of *this book is to highlight a comparative studies between developed and underdeveloped countries on the impact of policy making decisions and politics on education and business as Mohamed Sannoh recently discovered at Keele University in UK. Thorough analysis relating to tribalism, prolonged economic mismanagement by policy and decision makers in high places; especially within the politics since independent in 1961are reviewed to educate the new generation governments of Sierra Leone for the better. This book is funny and educative, though radical to the taste of politics of Sierra Leone and that's why Sierra Leonean politicians do not like reading it; but those who attempt taking that first step learn great joy to enjoy politics of change that we all look forward to.*

Abstract

Mohamed Sannoh

Mastering Business Administration in Education and African Politics (The Sierra Leone Chapter) has attracted my investment focus in education, especially at this time, more to explore how studies of the subject could help both wealth generation for Africa and how politics of the continent in general can help shape the movement to achieve. I am focusing on politics of Africa here because every achievement in every part of the continent is affected by the politics of the day in every country. One has to know how to "greet" politicians before things move.

In my native Sierra Leone, the buzzword of the day is "Who knows you" but even when it is for the benefit of those who are in need of education. The synoptic of "wusie den tie cow, na dae ie for eat" (where they tie cow is where it should graze) was the seed of corruption Siaka Stephens, the then president of APC regime sew during his hay days of unchallenged corruption. I was in charge of business educational programme which requires my signature to recommend deserving students to pursue further studies in the United Kingdom but the problems I had with my job forced me to close up and resettled in UK. The programme supporters had to suspend the operation because they felt that things were not moving in the right direction, especially economically, due to the politics of the day which I had no control over. After twenty five years of educational training and experience here in UK, I have discovered so much that Sierra Leone should now look into new investments that focus on boosting educational development which the politics of the day will live to consider seriously.

Mohamed Sannoh

PAGES OF ACADEDMIC INTERESTS: AFRICAN UNIVERSITIES

Why African Universities don't contest in the world's universities ranking is a crucial question baffling African academics but answered by Goolam Mohamedbhai, former Vice Chancellor of the University of Mauritius as published in the TES Higher by Phil Baty on 16 September 2010?

16th September 2010
By **Error! Hyperlink reference not valid.**

Africa's universities barely feature in the rankings. Some think that for them to even attempt to join the rankings race is a waste of resources that should be focused on improving lives in the communities they serve.

"African universities face enormous challenges," says Goolam Mohamedbhai. As a former secretary general of the Association of African Universities, former president of the International Association of Universities and acknowledged expert on higher education across the continent, he is well placed to make the assessment.

"Africa inherited a higher education system that was a carbon copy of [that of] the powers that colonised it. Right from the beginning, Africa started on a wrong footing—well behind the starting line, so to speak.

"Despite all the political and economic turmoil it has gone through since independence—often of its own making—it is now expected to compete on a completely non-level playing field. Not only is this unfair, it is also inappropriate," says Mohamedbhai, who has also served as vice-chancellor of the University of Mauritius.

"One could argue that other regions that were also colonised—South Asia, Latin America—are doing reasonably well. However, none of these regions suffered from the sort of exploitation that Africa underwent and continues to experience."

A *Global Research Report on Africa* produced by Thomson Reuters, *Times Higher Education's* data supplier for the World University Rankings, sets the context in dramatic terms.

Africa has more than 50 nations, hundreds of languages and a welter of ethnic cultural diversity, the report points out. It is a continent with abundant natural resources that is also plagued by the now-familiar litany of post-colonial woes: poverty, political instability, corruption, disease and armed conflicts frequently driven by ethnic and tribal divisions, the report says.

Its educational outlook as a whole looks bleak. More than half the continent is off course to meet or is relinquishing advances made towards the goal of ensuring universal primary education by 2015, Thomson Reuters says, and Africa has "haemorrhaged talent" for too long.

"Many of its best students take their higher degrees at universities in Europe, Asia and North America. Too few returns. The African diasporas provides powerful intellectual input to the research achievements of other countries but returns less benefit to the countries of birth," the report says.

"Science and technology are critical not only to the continent's economic prosperity but also to such matters as food security, disease control, access to clean water and environmental sustainability . . . The volume of [research] activity remains small, much smaller than is desirable if the potential contribution of Africa's researchers is to be realized for the benefit of its populations."

Chris Brink, vice-chancellor of Newcastle University in the UK and the former head of Stellenbosch University in South Africa, says that, with the exception of South Africa, "the trajectory of higher education in Africa, particularly sub-Sahara, is quite depressing, and the prognosis is not particularly good. Nor is the situation helped by the developed world mining Africa for human resources just as efficiently as it has been mining it for natural resources."

Martin Hall, vice-chancellor of the UK's University of Salford and a former deputy vice-chancellor of the University of Cape Town, says it is a "bitter irony" that "large numbers of talented academics from Africa have to pursue their careers in Europe and North America, where they make a significant contribution to the ranking and recognition of universities in these continents".

Across Africa in general, he says: "Universities have been chronically under-resourced for more than half a century, and they can often no longer afford books and journal subscriptions for their libraries.

"Academics working in these conditions hardly enjoy a level playing field in a game where the conventions of research and mutual recognition count for so much."

South Africa is the exception, the continent's one higher education bright spot. It has a system that can compete with the world's best: the University of Cape Town is ranked joint 107th among the global top 200 institutions.

"South Africa has, arguably, the continent's strongest higher education system, and it's not surprising that the University of Cape Town is in the top 200 again," Hall says. "But South Africa's universities also serve a society that is now one of the most unequal in the world, and this means that other universities in the country have missions that are vitally important for social and political mobility, and [pursuing these aims] will not result in the specific forms of recognition that are measured by world ranking systems."

As Mohamedbhai sees it, however, not even South Africa's current strength can be taken for granted.

"Why are only some universities in South Africa getting globally ranked?" he asks. "The answer lies again in the colonial attitude adopted during the apartheid years, when education was the prerogative of only the minority affluent white people.

"There is no doubt that South African higher education will soon be facing the same challenges that other African countries face. There is a serious shortage of PhDs and research output in Africa, with only a few universities producing high-level research while the others have no human and physical resources to do so."

In light of the continent's urgent problems, Mohamedbhai thinks that African universities should absent themselves from the race to rise up the rankings and focus their efforts on immediate needs.

"Do African universities need to be ranked globally? I don't think so. Their mission should be to produce the appropriate manpower required for Africa's development, to undertake research that is of direct relevance to Africa—which may not be acceptable for publication in the best scientific journals—and to reach out to assist the communities in the many challenges they are facing, especially poverty reduction.

"None of these fits the criteria used for global ranking. African universities have a duty to serve their countries and region first before seeking global glory. The tragedy is that many African governments, blinded by the prestige of global rankings, are challenging their universities to be ranked without understanding the consequences of the grossly inappropriate use of resources that that would entail.

"At the end of the day, this brings us back to the very purpose of higher education in a country. Not all universities in the world can have the same mission. Priorities are different in different countries, and universities must not be forced to conform to a single model of a world-class university."

Phil Baty
Subscribe to Times Higher Education

THE World University Rankings 2010 presented by Thomson Reuters

World Rank	Institution	Country / Region	Overall score change	Teaching change	International mix change	Industry income change	Research change	Citations change
1	Harvard University	United States	96.1	99.7	72.4	34.5	98.7	98.8
2	California Institute of Technology	United States	96.0	97.7	54.6	83.7	98.0	99.9
3	Massachusetts Institute of Technology	United States	95.6	97.8	82.3	87.5	91.4	99.9
4	Stanford University	United States	94.3	98.3	29.5	64.3	98.1	99.2
5	Princeton University	United States	94.2	90.9	70.3	Data not supplied	95.4	99.9
6	University of Cambridge	United Kingdom	91.2	90.5	77.7	57.0	94.1	94.0
6	University of Oxford	United Kingdom	91.2	88.2	77.2	73.5	93.9	95.1
8	University of California Berkeley	United States	91.1	84.2	39.6	Data not supplied	99.3	97.8
9	Imperial College London	United Kingdom	90.6	89.2	90.0	92.9	94.5	88.3
10	Yale University	United States	89.5	92.1	59.2	Data not supplied	89.7	91.5
11	University of California Los Angeles	United States	87.7	83.0	48.1	Data not supplied	92.9	93.2
12	University of Chicago	United States	86.9	79.1	62.8	Data not supplied	87.9	96.9
13	Johns Hopkins University	United States	86.4	80.9	58.5	100.0	89.2	92.3
14	Cornell University	United States	83.9	82.2	62.4	34.7	88.8	88.1
15	Swiss Federal Institute of Technology Zurich	Switzerland	83.4	77.5	93.7	Data not supplied	87.8	83.1
15	University of Michigan	United States	83.4	83.9	53.3	59.6	89.1	84.1
17	University of Toronto	Canada	82.0	75.8	Data not supplied	Data not supplied	87.9	82.2

THE World University Rankings 2010 presented by Thomson Reuters

World Rank	Institution	Country / Region	Overall score change	Teaching change	International mix change	Industry income change	Research change	Citations change
18	Columbia University	United States	81.0	73.8	90.9	Data not supplied	73.8	92.6
19	University of Pennsylvania	United States	79.5	71.8	32.9	43.7	82.7	93.6
20	Carnegie Mellon University	United States	79.3	70.3	39.1	53.7	79.3	95.7
21	University of Hong Kong	Hong Kong	79.2	68.4	91.4	56.5	71.4	96.1
22	University College London	United Kingdom	78.4	74.0	90.8	39.0	81.6	80.6
23	University of Washington	United States	78.0	68.2	49.0	32.8	77.1	95.9
24	Duke University	United States	76.5	66.8	49.4	100.0	71.5	92.3
25	Northwestern University	United States	75.9	64.5	60.5	Data not supplied	68.8	95.3
26	University of Tokyo	Japan	75.6	87.7	18.4	Data not supplied	91.9	58.1
27	Georgia Institute of Technology	United States	75.3	67.9	73.2	95.1	72.6	83.2
28	Pohang University of Science and Technology	Republic of Korea	75.1	69.5	32.6	100.0	62.5	96.5
29	University of California Santa Barbara	United States	75.0	56.6	64.3	89.8	68.0	98.8
30	University of British Columbia	Canada	73.8	65.1	93.3	42.6	74.8	80.3
30	University of North Carolina, Chapel Hill	United States	73.8	70.9	21.5	50.2	75.1	85.0
32	University of California San Diego	United States	73.2	59.8	31.6	51.8	76.3	90.8
33	University of Illinois—Urbana	United States	73.0	68.1	55.9	Data not supplied	80.9	72.9
34	National University of Singapore	Singapore	72.9	65.5	97.8	40.5	72.6	78.7
35	McGill University	Canada	71.7	69.0	85.9	Data not supplied	74.9	69.0

THE World University Rankings 2010 presented by Thomson Reuters

World Rank	Institution	Country / Region	Overall score change	Teaching change	International mix change	Industry income change	Research change	Citations change
36	University of Melbourne	Australia	71.0	58.7	88.0	47.7	69.2	83.3
37	Peking University	China	70.7	76.4	68.6	98.6	61.3	72.2
38	Washington University Saint Louis	United States	69.9	58.9	56.4	Data not supplied	63.0	88.6
39	Ecole Polytechnique	France	69.5	57.9	77.9	Data not supplied	56.1	91.4
40	University of Edinburgh	United Kingdom	69.2	59.9	67.3	42.2	61.9	86.8
41	Hong Kong University of Science and Technology	Hong Kong	69.0	50.4	97.4	64.1	51.8	98.2
42	Ecole Normale Superieure, Paris	France	68.6	66.8	44.9	30.7	48.2	95.7
43	Australian National University	Australia	67.0	51.9	93.9	Data not supplied	62.4	81.0
43	University of Göttingen	Germany	67.0	57.3	44.5	31.7	55.9	92.5
43	Karolinska Institute	Sweden	67.0	65.8	Data not supplied	73.3	72.7	62.3
43	University of Wisconsin	United States	67.0	55.5	43.7	Data not supplied	64.6	83.4
47	Rice University	United States	66.9	57.4	31.2	29.2	50.6	99.1
48	École Polytechnique Federale of Lausanne	Switzerland	66.5	55.0	100.0	38.0	56.1	83.8
49	University of Science and Technology of China	China	66.0	57.5	Data not supplied	30.3	48.6	92.7
49	University of California Irvine	United States	66.0	49.4	66.3	Data not supplied	54.7	91.6
51	Vanderbilt University	United States	65.9	64.9	22.1	84.2	59.5	78.1
52	University of Minnesota	United States	65.6	57.6	23.0	Data not supplied	69.1	76.4

THE World University Rankings 2010 presented by Thomson Reuters

World Rank	Institution	Country / Region	Overall score change	Teaching change	International mix change	Industry income change	Research change	Citations change
53	Tufts University	United States	65.2	64.1	28.3	Data not supplied	52.3	83.9
54	University of California Davis	United States	65.0	57.3	60.5	48.0	70.7	68.8
55	Brown University	United States	64.9	59.7	60.5	Data not supplied	57.0	77.7
56	University of Massachusetts	United States	64.7	61.3	22.6	53.9	72.6	67.9
57	Kyoto University	Japan	64.6	78.9	18.4	67.1	77.7	46.3
58	Tsinghua University	China	64.2	74.9	43.0	97.8	66.6	52.7
59	Boston University	United States	64.0	53.6	38.1	29.6	51.9	91.4
60	New York University	United States	63.9	62.0	31.8	Data not supplied	50.7	82.9
61	University of Munich	Germany	63.0	59.1	43.1	40.4	57.5	76.4
61	Emory University	United States	63.0	63.4	52.3	Data not supplied	48.4	77.8
63	University of Notre Dame	United States	62.8	56.4	35.6	Data not supplied	45.1	89.1
64	University of Pittsburgh	United States	62.7	58.5	25.2	37.9	58.3	78.3
65	Case Western Reserve University	United States	62.2	67.2	56.5	Data not supplied	53.8	66.0
66	Ohio State University	United States	62.1	63.5	64.0	Data not supplied	54.9	67.2
67	University of Colorado	United States	61.6	46.4	31.7	Data not supplied	58.1	83.4
68	University of Bristol	United Kingdom	61.4	49.6	67.2	36.2	53.1	80.9
68	University of California Santa Cruz	United States	61.4	38.3	16.7	Data not supplied	50.4	99.6
68	Yeshiva University	United States	61.4	63.5	53.3	Data not supplied	46.7	74.4
71	University of Sydney	Australia	61.2	49.8	89.6	90.8	61.9	64.3
72	University of Virginia	United States	61.1	62.0	42.2	Data not supplied	55.4	68.6

THE World University Rankings 2010 presented by Thomson Reuters

World Rank	Institution	Country / Region	Overall score change	Teaching change	International mix change	Industry income change	Research change	Citations change
73	University of Adelaide	Australia	60.7	46.5	87.5	52.7	38.8	90.5
73	University of Southern California	United States	60.7	65.4	31.2	Data not supplied	48.7	71.9
75	William & Mary	United States	60.4	53.1	20.9	Data not supplied	36.1	95.6
76	Trinity College Dublin	Ireland	60.3	47.7	84.2	31.6	45.3	84.4
77	King's College London	United Kingdom	59.7	48.5	85.9	44.1	54.5	72.1
78	Stony Brook University	United States	59.6	48.5	52.2	Data not supplied	43.6	85.8
79	Korea Advanced Institute of Science and Technology	Republic of Korea	59.5	71.3	36.7	100.0	63.4	45.5
79	University of Sussex	United Kingdom	59.5	42.4	72.8	29.1	42.4	91.6
81	University of Queensland Australia	Australia	59.1	51.8	74.2	57.1	53.4	69.0
81	University of York	United Kingdom	59.1	47.9	66.6	36.2	46.2	81.9
83	Ruprecht Karl University of Heidelberg	Germany	59.0	59.2	63.4	39.1	47.5	70.3
83	University of Utah	United States	59.0	55.8	22.5	Data not supplied	54.2	72.0
85	Durham University	United Kingdom	58.9	39.8	65.7	33.9	44.1	91.0
86	London School of Economics and Political Science	United Kingdom	58.3	62.4	99.5	38.4	56.2	51.6
87	University of Manchester	United Kingdom	58.0	56.5	79.1	39.0	56.2	59.2
88	Royal Holloway, University of London	United Kingdom	57.9	37.7	92.9	30.5	36.2	93.2
89	Lund University	Sweden	57.8	46.3	56.8	33.2	60.8	67.6
90	University of Zurich	Switzerland	57.7	56.6	87.9	43.8	47.0	65.0

THE World University Rankings 2010 presented by Thomson Reuters

World Rank	Institution	Country / Region	Overall score change	Teaching change	International mix change	Industry income change	Research change	Citations change
90	University of Southampton	United Kingdom	57.7	50.8	69.0	37.7	47.8	72.9
90	Wake Forest University	United States	57.7	54.6	24.4	Data not supplied	42.9	79.2
93	McMaster University	Canada	57.6	44.7	Data not supplied	Data not supplied	58.7	68.5
94	University College Dublin	Ireland	57.5	42.4	87.0	Data not supplied	36.6	86.3
95	University of Basel	Switzerland	57.3	50.2	91.3	45.8	37.1	78.3
95	George Washington University	United States	57.3	60.6	39.6	Data not supplied	43.1	70.2
95	University of Arizona	United States	57.3	52.4	21.9	84.2	52.2	70.1
98	University of Maryland College Park	United States	57.2	45.4	35.4	Data not supplied	48.6	79.2
99	Dartmouth College	United States	57.1	44.7	31.0	Data not supplied	49.2	79.7
100	ENS de Lyon	France	57.0	51.1	37.6	26.1	34.4	88.8
101	Technical University of Munich	Germany	56.9	50.4	85.3	Data not supplied	43.2	71.2
102	University of Helsinki	Finland	56.6	49.0	24.2	30.2	51.4	75.4
103	University of St. Andrews	United Kingdom	56.5	44.8	85.7	32.6	47.7	72.9
104	Rensselaer Polytechnic Institute	United States	56.4	50.5	48.0	Data not supplied	54.6	64.9
105	Rutgers the State University of New Jersey	United States	56.3	53.4	26.8	Data not supplied	64.7	55.7
106	Purdue University	United States	56.2	57.0	62.6	Data not supplied	67.8	43.9
107	University of Cape Town	South Africa	56.1	36.6	83.3	Data not supplied	42.1	82.8
107	National Tsing Hua University	Taiwan	56.1	52.2	34.1	50.2	52.6	66.9
109	Seoul National University	Republic of Korea	56.0	62.3	44.9	43.0	54.1	54.6

THE World University Rankings 2010 presented by Thomson Reuters

World Rank	Institution	Country / Region	Overall score change	Teaching change	International mix change	Industry income change	Research change	Citations change
109	Pennsylvania State University	United States	56.0	46.3	19.9	44.0	49.2	77.6
111	Hong Kong Baptist University	Hong Kong	55.6	32.9	71.8	26.7	32.5	97.6
112	Tokyo Institute of Technology	Japan	55.4	62.9	24.8	60.5	63.4	45.5
112	Bilkent University	Turkey	55.4	34.3	47.7	32.4	36.1	95.7
114	Eindhoven University of Technology	Netherlands	55.3	55.4	44.9	99.8	51.7	56.9
115	National Taiwan University	Taiwan	55.2	50.3	29.2	35.7	59.0	61.6
115	University of Hawaii	United States	55.2	38.3	34.2	Data not supplied	47.6	81.0
117	University of California Riverside	United States	55.1	38.6	63.0	30.5	47.4	78.3
118	University of Geneva	Switzerland	55.0	46.6	95.7	32.7	49.7	63.1
119	Catholic University of Leuven	Belgium	54.8	57.7	29.6	97.7	62.9	45.2
120	Nanjing University	China	54.6	52.2	50.2	43.4	46.2	66.0
120	Queen Mary, University of London	United Kingdom	54.6	39.7	91.0	38.9	44.1	73.5
122	Technical University of Denmark	Denmark	54.5	46.2	64.0	95.5	46.9	64.6
122	Michigan State University	United States	54.5	50.4	30.4	Data not supplied	52.7	63.7
124	Ghent University	Belgium	54.4	52.8	24.7	97.1	59.1	52.8
124	Leiden University	Netherlands	54.4	47.3	40.0	100.0	54.9	59.3
124	Lancaster University	United Kingdom	54.4	43.5	73.8	28.8	41.9	74.9
127	University of Alberta	Canada	54.3	53.7	71.6	44.5	58.0	49.7
128	University of Glasgow	United Kingdom	54.2	45.6	55.1	61.0	50.3	65.1
129	Stockholm University	Sweden	54.0	36.9	Data not supplied	31.7	49.2	75.9

THE World University Rankings 2010 presented by Thomson Reuters

World Rank	Institution	Country / Region	Overall score change	Teaching change	International mix change	Industry income change	Research change	Citations change
130	University of Victoria	Canada	53.4	32.9	Data not supplied	27.4	48.3	79.1
130	Osaka University	Japan	53.4	61.7	20.1	73.4	63.4	40.0
132	University of Freiburg	Germany	53.3	52.4	46.2	79.8	41.4	64.3
132	Tohoku University	Japan	53.3	60.3	20.1	82.3	62.5	41.2
132	University of Iowa	United States	53.3	48.6	31.7	Data not supplied	59.8	54.8
135	University of Bergen	Norway	52.7	39.9	66.6	41.5	42.1	73.1
136	University of Lausanne	Switzerland	52.6	43.1	84.1	42.5	50.5	59.1
137	University of Sheffield	United Kingdom	52.5	48.9	62.7	40.3	49.2	58.4
138	University of Montreal	Canada	52.4	56.1	Data not supplied	Data not supplied	49.4	51.9
139	VU University Amsterdam	Netherlands	52.3	47.6	30.6	81.4	51.6	58.5
140	Pierre and Marie Curie University	France	52.2	51.9	30.7	26.4	37.2	71.5
140	University of Dundee	United Kingdom	52.2	34.1	54.4	49.3	41.0	79.3
142	University of Barcelona	Spain	52.1	34.1	22.3	30.0	33.7	91.9
143	Utrecht University	Netherlands	52.0	43.4	52.6	55.3	53.0	58.8
144	Wageningen University and Research Center	Netherlands	51.9	58.5	24.3	Data not supplied	48.8	53.0
145	University of Auckland	New Zealand	51.8	34.8	94.3	61.1	39.2	71.8
145	University of Birmingham	United Kingdom	51.8	50.3	73.8	34.8	50.7	52.1
147	Alexandria University	Egypt	51.6	29.5	19.3	36.0	28.0	99.8
147	Uppsala University	Sweden	51.6	49.6	77.9	39.5	62.2	40.7
149	Hong Kong Polytechnic University	Hong Kong	51.4	39.4	82.9	57.2	45.7	62.4

THE World University Rankings 2010 presented by Thomson Reuters

World Rank	Institution	Country / Region	Overall score change	Teaching change	International mix change	Industry income change	Research change	Citations change
149	University of Aberdeen	United Kingdom	51.4	37.8	86.1	47.0	45.2	64.6
151	Delft University of Technology	Netherlands	51.3	55.5	47.4	99.4	67.7	29.0
152	University of New South Wales	Australia	51.2	49.5	70.7	60.0	48.9	51.2
152	Birkbeck, University of London	United Kingdom	51.2	41.2	88.5	27.4	35.8	70.6
152	Newcastle University	United Kingdom	51.2	42.7	80.5	31.1	42.8	63.6
155	Pompeu Fabra University	Spain	51.1	35.0	44.1	40.0	33.0	84.7
156	Indiana University	United States	51.0	48.5	37.7	Data not supplied	42.5	63.2
156	Iowa State University	United States	51.0	49.3	23.2	49.6	49.6	58.2
158	Medical College of Georgia	United States	50.7	67.3	16.3	50.1	41.7	48.9
159	Erasmus University Rotterdam	Netherlands	50.4	39.4	58.6	Data not supplied	43.6	65.5
159	University of Delaware	United States	50.4	38.4	16.8	100.0	51.9	61.3
161	Arizona State University	United States	50.3	43.0	24.1	Data not supplied	44.1	66.9
161	Boston College	United States	50.3	40.1	31.6	Data not supplied	33.6	78.0
163	National Sun Yat-Sen University	Taiwan	50.2	46.1	21.3	37.5	50.6	58.9
164	Georgetown University	United States	50.1	65.1	24.7	Data not supplied	44.7	45.0
165	University of Amsterdam	Netherlands	50.0	42.5	38.2	38.8	49.2	60.2
165	University of Liverpool	United Kingdom	50.0	40.8	59.8	40.6	47.8	59.6
167	Aarhus University	Denmark	49.9	38.1	33.4	61.5	55.6	57.3
168	University of Würzburg	Germany	49.8	48.7	40.3	Data not supplied	40.9	60.4

THE World University Rankings 2010 presented by Thomson Reuters

World Rank	Institution	Country / Region	Overall score change	Teaching change	International mix change	Industry income change	Research change	Citations change
168	University of Leeds	United Kingdom	49.8	46.2	50.0	38.3	48.0	55.6
170	University of Groningen	Netherlands	49.7	41.7	35.5	34.2	56.4	54.1
171	Sun Yat-sen University	China	49.6	46.2	29.3	41.2	34.7	70.2
172	Johann Wolfgang Goethe University Frankfurt am Main	Germany	49.4	39.2	56.1	41.6	37.3	69.5
173	Bielefeld University	Germany	49.3	39.9	Data not supplied	Data not supplied	35.7	70.4
174	Nanyang Technological University	Singapore	49.0	43.6	96.3	40.0	51.7	45.0
174	University of East Anglia	United Kingdom	49.0	42.1	62.8	29.7	40.4	62.8
174	University of Nottingham	United Kingdom	49.0	46.8	74.8	38.4	44.1	52.5
177	University of Copenhagen	Denmark	48.8	44.1	45.8	26.1	45.7	58.3
178	Monash University	Australia	48.5	39.4	87.1	40.8	38.8	60.5
178	Humboldt University of Berlin	Germany	48.5	50.9	46.1	27.8	44.5	52.0
178	University of Bonn	Germany	48.5	46.8	46.8	29.4	33.8	65.3
181	National Chiao Tung University	Taiwan	48.3	53.2	57.9	98.7	54.4	32.9
182	RWTH Aachen University	Germany	48.2	50.0	63.8	56.6	42.5	48.9
183	Middle East Technical University	Turkey	47.7	39.5	27.2	43.9	39.5	66.4
184	University of Exeter	United Kingdom	47.6	40.4	62.8	32.2	42.5	57.9
185	University of Twente	Netherlands	47.5	49.9	62.4	49.8	48.3	42.0
186	University of Konstanz	Germany	47.3	42.7	93.6	Data not supplied	40.1	51.3

THE World University Rankings 2010 presented by Thomson Reuters

World Rank	Institution	Country / Region	Overall score change	Teaching change	International mix change	Industry income change	Research change	Citations change
187	University of Innsbruck	Austria	47.2	37.9	99.5	35.0	34.8	60.2
187	Karlsruhe Institute of Technology	Germany	47.2	45.0	47.3	40.0	35.4	60.7
189	Eberhard Karls University, Tübingen	Germany	47.0	45.9	57.8	32.3	36.3	57.3
190	Yonsei University	Republic of Korea	46.9	43.0	28.0	40.4	48.7	52.2
190	Drexel University	United States	46.9	45.0	60.6	27.4	35.9	58.2
190	University of Cincinnati	United States	46.9	43.6	18.9	32.5	40.4	61.5
193	Dalhousie University	Canada	46.8	41.6	44.9	Data not supplied	50.2	48.8
193	Royal Institute of Technology	Sweden	46.8	49.1	64.2	100.0	56.2	29.2
195	University of Vienna	Austria	46.7	47.6	63.2	27.0	45.7	45.6
196	Kent State University	United States	46.5	33.5	15.9	26.3	33.3	76.8
197	Zhejiang University	China	46.4	54.6	29.6	70.3	41.3	44.3
197	University of Illinois—Chicago	United States	46.4	57.8	51.8	Data not supplied	46.8	34.7
199	Simon Fraser University	Canada	46.2	32.9	51.9	37.9	44.2	60.2
199	Swedish University of Agricultural Sciences	Sweden	46.2	43.3	Data not supplied	99.9	49.5	41.7

Editor's note.

A key principle of our revised rankings system in its first year is that it includes only institutions that have assented to join the profiling process and have provided and verified the data we sought.

Unfortunately, when the rankings list was published in September 2010, the University of Oslo contacted Times Higher Education to inform us that, because of an error on its part and an oversight in the data quality-control process, some of the data it supplied were incorrect.

A reanalysis of the data by Thomson Reuters has found that Oslo would have been ranked at 186th in the world.

Also, after the launch of the World University Rankings 2010 it became apparent that, owing to a data processing error, the ranking positions of two Australian universities in the top 200 list were incorrect — the University of Adelaide and Monash University.

Both universities remain in the top 1 per cent of world universities.

Thomson Reuters regrets this error and any impact this issue has on the institutions involved as well as on Times Higher Education. Thomson Reuters has taken corrective action to ensure that these errors will not be repeated. Thomson Reuters and Times Higher Education sincerely apologise.

Phil Baty

Contact us: rankings@timeshighereducation.co.uk
Keep informed: join Times Higher Education's mailing list
Subscribe to Times Higher Education
Times Higher Education World University Rankings on Facebook
Times Higher Education World University Rankings on Twitter

Universities in the UK, listed in alphabetical order:

A

1. University of Aberdeen
2. University of Abertay Dundee
3. Aberystwyth University
4. Anglia Ruskin University
5. Armagh Observatory
6. Arts University College at Bournemouth
7. University of the Arts London
8. Aston University, Birmingham

B

1. Bangor University
2. Bath Spa University
3. University of Bath
4. University of Bedfordshire
5. Birkbeck, University of London
6. Birmingham City University
7. University of Birmingham
8. University College Birmingham
9. Bishop Grosseteste University College Lincoln
10. University of Bolton
11. Bournemouth University
12. University of Bradford
13. Brighton and Sussex Medical School
14. University of Brighton
15. University of Bristol
16. British Institute in Paris

17. Brunel University
18. University of Buckingham
19. Bucks New University

C

1. University of Cambridge
2. Canterbury Christ Church University
3. Cardiff University
4. University of Wales Institute, Cardiff
5. University of Central Lancashire
6. Central School of Speech & Drama, University of London
7. University of Wales Centre for Advanced Welsh and Celtic Studies
8. University of Chester
9. University of Chichester
10. City University London
11. Conservatoire for Dance and Drama
12. The Courtauld Institute of Art
13. Coventry University
14. Cranfield University
15. University for the Creative Arts
16. University of Cumbria

D

1. De Montfort University
2. University of Derby
3. University of Dundee
4. Durham University

E

1. University of East Anglia
2. University of East London
3. Edge Hill University
4. Edinburgh College of Art
5. Edinburgh Napier University
6. University of Edinburgh
7. University of Essex
8. University of Exeter

F

1. University College Falmouth

G

1. University of Glamorgan
2. Glasgow Caledonian University
3. Glasgow School of Art
4. University of Glasgow
5. University of Gloucestershire
6. Glyndŵr University
7. Goldsmiths, University of London
8. University of Greenwich
9. Guildhall School of Music & Drama

H

1. Harper Adams University College
2. Heriot-Watt University
3. University of Hertfordshire
4. Heythrop College

13. London Business School
14. London Metropolitan University
15. London School of Economics and Political Science
16. London School of Hygiene & Tropical Medicine
17. London South Bank University
18. Loughborough University

M

1. Manchester Metropolitan University
2. Manchester School of Architecture
3. University of Manchester
4. Middlesex University

N

1. Newcastle University
2. Newman University College, Birmingham
3. University of Wales, Newport
4. University of Northampton
5. Northumbria University
6. Norwich University College of the Arts
7. Nottingham Trent University
8. University of Nottingham

O

1. Open University
2. Oxford Brookes University
3. University of Oxford

P

1. University of Plymouth
2. University College Plymouth St Mark and St John
3. University of Portsmouth

Q

1. Queen Margaret University, Edinburgh
2. Queen Mary, University of London
3. Queen's University Belfast

R

1. Ravensbourne
2. University of Reading
3. Robert Gordon University
4. Roehampton University
5. Rose Bruford College
6. Royal Academy of Music
7. Royal Agricultural College
8. Royal College of Art
9. Royal College of Music
10. Royal Conservatoire of Scotland
11. Royal Holloway, University of London
12. Royal Northern College of Music
13. Royal Veterinary College
14. Royal Welsh College of Music and Drama

S

1. University of Salford
2. School of Oriental and African Studies
3. School of Pharmacy, University of London
4. Scottish Agricultural College
5. Sheffield Hallam University
6. University of Sheffield
7. University of Southampton
8. Southampton Solent University
9. Southbank University, London
10. University of St Andrews
11. St George's, University of London
12. St Mary's University College, Belfast
13. St Mary's University College, Twickenham
14. Staffordshire University
15. University of Stirling
16. Stranmillis University College
17. University of Strathclyde
18. University Campus Suffolk
19. University of Sunderland
20. University of Surrey
21. University of Sussex
22. Swansea Metropolitan University
23. Swansea University

T

1. Teesside University
2. Trinity Laban Conservatoire of Music and Dance
3. University of Wales, Trinity St David

U

1. University of Ulster
2. University Marine Biological Station, Millport
3. CL (University College London)

W

1. University of Warwick
2. University of West London
3. University of the West of England
4. University of the West of Scotland
5. University of Westminster
6. University of Winchester
7. University of Wolverhampton
8. University of Worcester
9. Writtle College

Y

1. York St John University
2. University of York

Contents

Quotable Quote

"I am a businessman with lot of business experience. I have managed my own business in the past successfully. That business is the National Insurance Company.

I am going to run this country like a business organisation and to make sure that the profit is declared to its shareholders.

First of all, I am going to embark on fighting corruption in this country. All those who have been in positions in this country in the past government including former Vice President Solomon Ekuma Mberewa will have to give account of their stewardship for the past five years before they go.

As of now, no one is allowed to leave this country until I say so. I am going to set up anticorruption department and they are going to be very vigilant with their work." President Ernest Bai Koroma, of the Republic of Sierra Leone (2007).

But can business philosophy be applied in the place of politics to make sense? Let's wait and see how Ernest Koroma does it.

Acknowledgements

The completion of this book would not have reached without the painstaking of constantly reminding me of coursework submission deadline date by Dorothy Tyson, MBA course administrator at the University of Keele who also showed tremendous understanding for my illness of (high blood pressure that resulted into mild stroke) during the course and the required extensions that enabled me to complete.

Special gratitude is extended to my through the pages of this book for her supports, humanly possible that kept me going, despite the hot arguments at home.

Mr. Samuel Jonjo is my long time friend dated as far back as our teaching days in Sierra Leone who later became more interested in politics. At one time, he occupied the office of the Leader of the Sierra Leone Peoples Party (SLPP) in the United Kingdom and the Northern Ireland. Also as founder of "Friends of Solomon Berewa", I personally admired his loyalty and supports for the then Vice President of Sierra Loene until his conceit of defeat to Ernest Bai Koroma of the then opposition, The All Peoples Congress (APC) during the 2007 general elections of Sierra Leone, a new chapter in the political history of that country. I had the privilege of receiving his time and attention for proof reading and advising on some of the political facts established here on Sierra Leone. As far as my memory goes, Mr. Samuel Jonjo is yet the most serious of the SLPP supporters, next to Late Pa Mana Kpaka and I wish him well in his future presidential role of the Republic of Sierra Leone, although I would not personally accept a ministerial appointment from his office because he knows fully well that politics is not just my cup of tea. I hope he will learn from my discoveries in this book.

Mr. Idris Mansaray, another close friend and former student from my teaching days in The Gambia is another academic enthusiast with MBA of Leicester University in UK. He had the pleasure of reading the manuscript of this book with his suggestions and contributions arriving just in time.

Mr. Willie O. Pratt was my Vice Principal, Principal and colleague at the Methodist Boys High School in Freetown-Sierra Leone and I thank him for approving my study leave "with pay" to travel to the UK for further studies.

Let me send my thank you message to reach him successfully through the pages of this book.

Mamma Amie sells bread and beans acara (one-bread-two) and Mamma Marie Abu sells ginger beer which kept me surviving throughout the 1970s at the Methodist Boys' High School. God always bless them wherever they are.

My school friends were many but those I respected most for being gentle, more civilised and were not in anyway "Creolistic" and accepted me as a country-boy in their mist, (although some call me Mendeh-boy, in tribal-attack among the Creole boys) were Sheku Kai-kai, Herbert Coker, George Springsbury Williams, Samuel Greywood, Ishmael Dyfan, Hassan Bangura, Mustard Collier, George Shepherd, Babatunde Roland May, Nathaniel Peers, Braima Mendy, Maurice Nicol, George Betts, Patrick John, Komba Lansana, Komba Tondoneh, Kpanga Bonah, Roy Macauley, Lashite Beckley, Sulay Daramy, Harry John, Joko Toby, Athanatoius Sannah, Raymond Pratt, Donald Mark, Isiaka Harding, Daniel Kai-kai, John Collier, Hudson Maddy, Aquila Johnson, Vivian Nelson-Streeter, Bainga Kebbay, Ahmed Serray-Wurrie, Yamoh Conteh, Abdul Sindeh, Davidson Jonah, John Conteh, Samuel Kayodeh, Lamin Sippo Vandi, Mohamed Dukulay, Rudolph George, Samuel

George, Cyril Joxton-Smith, Pabs-Ganon, etc. (to name but just a few). Although some are now occupying high strategic positions in Sierra Leone and abroad, may the souls of those who have gone beyond rest in perfect peace until we meet again.

My teachers in those years were very great and their contributions to my life success will never go unnoticed but some that still remain dearest to my heart includes Miss Yatta Tejan-Kella (the 7 for 7 of Kenema town), Miss Fatmata Kai-kai, Mrs. Selina Ade-Williams, Miss Roseniour, Mr. C.J.Budkin, Mr. Williams, Mr. Johnson, Mr. Adams, Mr. Dumbuya, Claud Sewoh, Emanuel O. Grant (Toshman), Miss Olivia Walker, Mrs. Sylvia Akiwumi, Mr. Mohamed Yoki, Mrs. Agatha Ashley, Mr. Morgan, Mr.pabs-Ganon, Miss Sawyer, Bussar Tucker, Mr. Garber, etc.

"Labouramus Exspectantes".

MODULE ONE

Organisational Behaviour And Development

Assignment Title:

Drawing on appropriate literature, critically examine and discuss any two concepts or issues within organizational behavior. Examples might includes culture, leadership, gender, motivation, managing change, power and control, trust, professionalism, performativity. In structuring your essay, you should pay particular attention to the following <u>assessment criteria:</u>

1. *Explore and evaluate theories and concepts from a critical perspective*
2. *Connect theories with contemporary debates and issues in education management*
3. *Discuss how theories may be used as analytical tools to inform changes in management practice*
4. *Reflect upon your own professional practice and experience of management and organisations when locating your discussion.*
5. *Demonstrate understanding of current debates in educational management and practice.*
6. *Show linkages between the two concepts or theories under discussion.*

Assignment length: 3,000-3,500 words.

Some behavioural issues relating to culture and causes of change in educational organisations in the United Kingdom

Abstract and Introduction:

This assignment is a literature review, about how organisational behaviour applies to educational organisations, focusing on UK institutions. Although the number of words allowed is not sufficient to exhaust this research, I will attempt to highlight major issues to establish meaningful understanding about the topic under investigation.

Educational institutions in UK today, like all other business organisations are facing both external and internal forces that make change inevitable. Rising costs of management, demands of employee morale, need for efficiency, requirements for new products and services development, customer satisfaction triggered by high level of competition for students markets (overseas students who pay higher fees) and research grants from government and industries are jointly forcing cultural change and readjustment in UK educational institutions, be it for survival or growth.

Culture is a way of life and interprets human behaviour such as the practice of beliefs, faiths, communications, dress, values, food, relationship, acceptability, respect, leadership, the law, etc. Organisational culture therefore attempts to practice what the founders of the organisation originally had in mind at the time of commencement as stated in their mission statement. Nevertheless, does the letter always follow mission statements strictly? If it does not either consciously or unconsciously however, the effects of causes of change and shifts in organisational culture begin to emerge.

This research discovers that educational organisations (not only in UK) tend to change and further adopt different organisational behavioural patterns, primarily because of external pressures rather than internal desire or need to change. Organisations by themselves do not behave but the human elements responsible for the organisation triggered by changes determine the way organisations behave.

Change on the overall, in any organisation is a necessity for progress and adjustment to the needs of time and according to the requirements of customer satisfaction. As almost all UK educational organisations receive government sponsorship for their survival and progress, they are of no exemption to this rule. Where political debates highly influence or perhaps dictate the manner in which educational institutions behave, change is therefore educational organisations culture as investigated in this assignment.

Personal experience in vocational education management and suggestions for improvement in vocational education designs are provided in this assignment.

(Morgan, 2006) attempts to present organisational leaders with a set of models and theories that seek to empower and help with a way of thinking to motivate and address some of the ambiguity and flux in organisational behaviour.

Although Morgan highly discussed the usual approach of organisational leaders by being aware of and appreciating changes of organisational behaviour as they occur, he further explained that skilled organisational leaders usually develop the habits of understanding difficult scenarios in mind and thus enabling them to take appropriate actions. Derek Pugh's presentation of the definition of organisational behaviour by (Huczynski and Buchanan, 2007) as "the study of the structure, functioning and performance of organisations and the behaviour of groups and individuals within them" is highly reflected in Morgan's work on the subject.

However, Morgan's scepticism with this approach of organisational reading is that less effective managers and problem solvers would find the practice as fixed stand point and when faced with stumbling blocks, they cannot get around because the practice often turn managers and leaders into developing behavioural patterns that are rigid and inflexible.

As organisations always expect adjustment to prevailing circumstances triggered by needs to change, (Morrison, 1998) as recognised in his definition says that

> *"change can be regarded as a dynamic and continuous process of development and growth that involves a reorganisation in response to felt needs. It is a process of transformation, a flow from one state to another, either initiated by internal factors or external forces, involving individuals, groups or institutions, leading to a realignment of existing values, practices and outcomes".*

In his search to explore different methods of reading and understanding organisational life, Morgan discovered *"that all theories of organisations and management are based on implicit images or metaphors that lead us to see, understand and manage organisations in distinctive yet partial ways".*

Metaphor evades our imagination to enable us to perceive and develop specific way of thinking and seeing our environment, individuals and organisations we deal with on a day-to-day basis and relating them to what we imagine they are. *"my boss is a lion",* for example is perceived as such, not because he has sharp teeth, covered in fur, but we draw attention to his lion like behaviour or perhaps posture and body shape.

The caution to metaphor however, is that it distorts the true meaning or imagination of others although it stretches imagination in a way that can create powerful insights. Metaphor always produces a kind of one-sided approach.

Where metaphorically (my boss is a lion, others can also see him as pig or a devil). Metaphor therefore is a constructive falsehood and if taken literally, becomes ludicrous. It exaggerates and invites us to see the tiny similarities but ignore the greater differences.

Understanding of metaphor therefore puts us in a learning position to appreciate that there is no perfect single theory for organisational management but the main challenge lies in developing skills in the art of using metaphor which basically involves fresh ways of seeing, understanding and shaping the situations that we want to lead.

Organisational leaders are presented with the following concepts of metaphors; Gareth Morgan refers to as 'Images of Organisation' describing the evolution of different organisational structures and reflections of their different styles of management and leadership.

Morgan's work provides a major literature and in addition to others, used as theoretical base for the presentation of this paper focusing on the concepts of culture and managing change relating to some of the debates on educational management or leadership in the United Kingdom.

(Morgan, 2006) discusses that the behavioural pattern of some organisations is like machine, referring to bureaucratic organisations *designed to allow workers to participate in the whole production process only at a specific position they are assigned to operate with a well defined work role.* Including (Smith, 1776) in Wealth of Nations,

Morgan's view on mechanisation of labour received total support for the implementation of 'division of labour' at the factory floor.

The benefits of mechanisation as experienced relates to *'form of organisation that emphasises precision, speed, clarity, regularity, reliability and efficiency achieved through the creation of a fixed division of tasks, hierarchical supervision and detailed rules and regulations.'*

How has this reflected on settings of educational institutions in UK? Schools have the traditional approach to learning through the academic route ensuring that pupils are taught and prepared to pass examinations. Some of the subjects may not be useful to them in their working life. Teachers also have the tradition of gaining promotion through length of service, to departmental heads, senior teachers and eventually, head teacher status.

In the interest of improvement for schools and student learning however, understanding of the links between all parties including school, schooling and school leadership is very essential as suggested by (Brundrett et al, 2006).

This is done by identifying and relating outcomes of students learning gained from the curriculum through methods and process of teaching, availability and use of teaching aids such as information technology equipments (soft wares and hard wares), audiovisual (video or DVD films, documentaries), reference resources of relevant books, quality of teachers, organisational structures, financial resources and so on. All these may help towards building organisational culture within institutions.

Although mechanisation system may have positive effect on organisations, the approach may be devastating to some organisations of different image. Challenges about the system began to emerge when (Babbage, 1832) one of the earliest inventors of mathematical computers, advocated for a *'scientific'* approach to organisational management.

Heavily focused on *planning and appropriate division of labour and its importance to organisations and management,* his ideas gradually gained momentum within other circles of interest and then received the endorsement of a German sociologist, (Webber, 1947) whose main *concern was the consequences and effects of mechanisation on the human side of society.*

He saw mechanisation of human life as not only exploiting but also, the potential undermining and erosion effect of the spiritual side of human life and further increase of the capacity for spontaneous action, which might lead to future irrational behaviour.

Referring to the Japanese models of work, (Morrison, 1998) also raised concern on human cost of work and further sited the work of (Kamata, 1983) who elucidated on the exploitative condition in which employees are required to work; explaining that workers pay at Toyota, for example is too low. The work is too intense, too onerous work shifts system, unfriendly personnel practices and workers cannot easily afford to avoid sacrificing holiday for overtime work. Still sited by (Morrison, 1998), the 'Intensification Thesis' of (Hargreaves, 1994) raised the alarm that teachers' work are running into the danger of being regarded as exploitable operatives and that their working environment are becoming very stressful. Political interference sometimes results into dictating strongly, the manner in which teachers should conduct themselves and associate with students, which are becoming stressful and causing failures.

These have put some professionally trained and qualified teachers into the dilemma of how to perform exactly in the classroom during learning contacts periods, the time vital to the purpose of schooling. (Whitehead, 2005) of Keele University, observed the damages of political interference into educational management when he referred to the December 2004 Office for Standards in Education (Ofsted) report on further education colleges. Accordingly, 45 of 307 FE colleges inspected between April 2001 and June 2004 were failing because they focussed heavily on 'processes and procedures' which was in fact Ofsted imposed requirement, rather than focusing on developing strategies aiming at the outcomes of education to learners.

Other theorists such as F. W. Mooney, Col. Lyndall Urwick and Henri Fayol (Morgan, 2006) says, heavily put, scientific management approach under attack and suggested its replacement with the 'classical' style. They collectively defined management as *'a process of planning, organising, commanding, co-ordinating and controlling'* marking the foundation for modern management techniques such as management by objective **(MBO)** and planning, programming, budgeting systems **(PPBS).**

While the requirement for Qualified Teaching Status, (QTS) is mandatory for UK teachers in primary and secondary schools, (Brundrett et al, 2006) explains that head teacher status requirement in UK since 2004, now demands the award of National Professional Qualification for Headship (NPQH) introduced by the New Labour Government. Professional exchange visits and conferencing among educators have emerged and now practical among school leaders in different shapes such as taking project overseas. Sponsorships of visits of school leaders from overseas are now provided by National College for School Leadership (NCSL), also a New Labour initiative in England to share international best practice with their UK colleagues.

Morgan looks at **organisations as organisms** with a different image provoking organisational leaders to think and to see clearly that organisations experience metamorphosis just as living organisms and can adapt to changing circumstances as dictated by their environment; they are born and they can grow, develop, decline and die. Understanding this system, educates organisational leaders to cater for organisational needs accordingly if they are to survive and stay alive enough to produce profitably. (Brown's, 2005) explanation of the metamorphosis of education and learning in UK, especially in compulsory schooling (between the ages of 5 and 16) identifies major and changing social issue of great significance. The **tripartite** system of 'post primary' secondary schooling of the 11+ **(grammar, technical and secondary modern)** once operated in UK, came under heavy attack in the 1960s because it was seen to be practicing segregation and recipe for not only disadvantaging but also undermining confidence for success in life of children from working class background.

"Research in the 1950s and 1960s suggested that the talent, ability and potential for many children in secondary modern schools were being wasted. It was felt that this wasted talent could be better developed in comprehensive schools, which accept pupils of all abilities. As a result, in the 1960s the tripartite system was abolished in most of the country, and by the 1970s most children attended comprehensive schools," Brown says.

The abolition of the tripartite system and the emergence of comprehensive schools in UK produced significance benefits for educational achievements:

Educational success and obtaining qualifications remains open throughout in school career of some children because comprehensive schools provided better opportunities for late developers.

Large size of comprehensive schools catered for many learning opportunities including many teachers, wider variety of subjects of interest, learning equipments and facilities combined together in enabling the many to gaining qualifications who would have otherwise resulted into frustrated school dropout.

Comprehensive school system brought children of different social background (working class or upper class-rich or poor) together to learn to accept each other at early stages of life with mutual respect for each other's contribution to society and this helped greatly to reconstruct more decent social structure.

Key aims of educational change as quoted from Brown (2005) produced:

- *Economic efficiency by developing the talents of young people to improve the skills of the labour force so Britain maintains a successful position in the world economy.*
- *Making the education system meet the needs of industry and employers through more emphasis on vocational education.*
- *Raising educational standards.*
- *Creating equality of educational opportunity in a meritocratic society, and establishing a fairer society by opening up opportunities for secondary and further/higher education to the working class and other disadvantaged groups.*

Despite these developments realised by changes in education, the other significant importance relates to standard of education in Britain, as compared to other parts in Europe. According to a Polish reporter:

> *". . . Schools in Great Britain vary greatly in their teaching standards. That is another reason why Polish pupils and their friends from neighbouring countries get bored in the*

classroom-they attend schools with lower standards. The level
of teaching in primary and secondary schools is pretty-low,
assesses Zofia Kluk, whose son Patryk is in the seventh
grade. If you compare the maths schedule being studied here
with the one back in Poland it differs greatly. Even though
my son is in the highest set, he is bored during lessons . . ."
(Sepek, 2008) and further elucidated that kids are taught in
British schools with basic preparation techniques, how to do
project work, debating skills, how to defend their opinions
and are generally encouraged to get to know themselves.
British schools enable kids to recognise their potential and
develop their talents.

Fewer subjects are covered in schools but studied more in detail with
thorough understanding. Great Britain, being an island, practices a
different culture with a unique historical background different from the
rest of Europe, causing them to have little interest in teaching subjects
that are of no direct relevance to them even though they may be of
interest to other parts of Europe.

Although children learn narrowly in Britain according to the Polish
report, **they take it seriously.** They take more responsibility for their
fate and they have access to career advisors or guidance councilors
with whom they discuss what they want to do with their lives in future.
16+ year olds in British schools are matured enough to consider their
areas of degrees which guides them into selecting subjects for their
GCSEs and A' Levels.

Leadership as distributed concept, again forwarded by (Brundrett, et al
2006) explains that the head teacher or principal in schools nowadays
share leadership roles and responsibilities with every staff in schools,
hence leading to the eradication of underperformance.

Breaking head teacher's monopoly of leadership as professional development initiative referred to as Leading from the Middle, a programme at National College of School Leadership (NCSL) in England, further gave birth to additional innovation and benefits such as increase in staff motivation, boosting of morale, reduction of pressure and dismissal of unnecessary tension at learning organisational environment.

As (Daft, 2003) puts it, "change is any alteration in an organisation's structure, process or personnel" which can be threatening to some individuals in organisations. Organisational change as further elaborated is the process of adopting new ideas or behaviours by an organisation.

This can also apply to educational institutions, which further demands effective management practice. Organisations now face both external and internal forces (rising costs, employee morale, customer satisfaction, new products and services development and competition). In this era of globalisation, organisational change is inevitable.

Another demand placed on organisational change is the expectation to produce innovation so that the organisation is positioned in a leading role competitive advantage.

Effecting change is not always easy in organisations especially when the people associated with the organisation do not welcome the idea of change. According to (Kotter and Schlesinger 1979), there are four main reasons why certain people resist change:

i. *misunderstanding—communication problems and inadequate information make it impossible for people concerned to see the vision and clearly understand why.*

ii. *low tolerance to change—some employees are very keen on security and stability of their work and to what extent could this be affected by change.*

iii. *practical self-interest—some people are more concerned with the implications of the change for themselves and how it may affect their own interests rather than considering the effects on the success of the business.*

iv. *different assessment of the situation—some employees may disagree with the reasons for the change and also on the advantages and disadvantages of the strategy.*

There are different models of change. The most familiar and widely used model for change is the (Kurt Lewin, 1951) three-phase models of change including: unfreeze, move (or change) and refreeze. This model became the foundation of the development of 'Force Field Analysis' used to clarify those factors or driving forces that create a pressure for change and those restraining forces that create pressure against change.

Lewin explains that the first step towards change is to unfreeze the present pattern of behaviour as a way of management resistance to change. Depending on the organisational level of change intended, such unfreezing might involve: on the individual level (selectively promoting or terminating employees); on the structural level (developing highly experiential training programmes) and all of these are intended for organisational members to address levels and areas needed for change and prepare open mindedness approach for all change associates.

The second step, movement involves making the actual changes that will move the organisation to another response.

The final stage of the change process is refreezing where the recruitment and selection process redesigned with the view of increasing the likelihood or hiring applicants who share the organisation's new management style and value system.

From a practical professional experience, I was able to change and totally transform the education system of the Institute of Professional Administration & Management (IPAM) in the West African state of The Gambia, from internally assessed educational qualification system to externally assessed professional qualification programme, awarded by the Institute of Commercial Management (ICM) in the United Kingdom. The initiative further generated strong source of income for ICM through payments of registration and examination fees.

When I occupied office as Principal & Director of Education in this Sierra Leonean refugee institution in 2001-2004, my major determination was to provide students with qualifications of international recognition and further, to create higher status recognition of the institution locally for marketing purposes through change strategies recommended by (Beer et al 1990) as follows:

Commitment strategy—I diagnosed the institution's existing problem, which was lack of financially supports that prevented refugees from taking external examinations.

Co-ordination strategy—Some teachers (professional university graduates) at IPAM were providing voluntary services, who were themselves, refugees from Sierra Leone. Co-ordination between students and teachers were although somehow good, but commitment to service was not very strong.

A projected proposal, I forwarded to the United Nations High Commission for Refugees (UNHCR) for funding, was successful which enabled students to study free with their external examination fees paid to ICM and teachers placed on financial remuneration on teaching sessions. Staffs that are more qualified were recruited and those less qualified, advised to pursue further studies at half salaries.

This refugee programme became attractive to the non refugees of Gambia nationals who started applying for places to study for the British ICM Certificate and Diploma awards They were charged fees but still less than fees charged at the Gambia colleges.

Empowered and educated work force—The IPAM project would not have been successful without educated and dedicated staff combined with students who determined to take advantage of free education opportunities they received.

Communication—Cordial and open communication system (though professional) existed between staff and students during this transition period which highly contributed to success.

(Bush, 2003) refers to (Bolan's, 1999) definition of educational management as 'an executive function for carrying out agreed policy' and further differentiates educational leadership as having 'at its core the responsibility for policy formulation and, where appropriate, organisational transformation'. Bush further elaborated by sitting (Glatter's, 1979) definition which serves to identify the scope of the subject by explaining that management studies are concerned with *'the internal operation of educational institutions, and also with their relationships with their environment, that is, the communities in which they are set, and with the governing bodies to which they are formally responsible'.*

In their leadership roles, therefore, managers in educational institutions are faced with both internal and external audiences and thus identifying the boundaries of educational management.

In this world of globalisation and especially when educational institutions (post secondary in particular) are scouting for students and research projects worldwide, to what extent could educational boundaries be measured by UK based institutions?

Some of these questions are somehow, addressed by (Morgan, 2006) who further explains the metaphor of *organisations as culture* referring to the pattern of development reflected in a society's system of knowledge, ideology, values, laws and daily activities. Understanding the fact that different groups of people have different ways of life, helps organisational leaders further to understand cross-national variations in organisation and target markets.

Finally, employers are now-a-days much interested in graduates or candidates for employments, with some amount of working experience or at least, apprenticeship placement background gained during the course of studies. Therefore, educational delivery systems, especially for vocational qualifications are bound to change in order to satisfy the requirements of employers.

Training colleges, as strong recommendation, in their preparation of students for work or promotions should focus on improving performance standards through consistent research, development and teaching the vocational skills specifically meant for satisfying needs of employers in the public and private sector organisations.

In addition to subjects' knowledge, vocational course designs should endeavour to assist students to develop interpersonal skills relating to team working, leadership, communication and presentation skills. As (Beeden, 2008) of Hope Valley College, Derbyshire agrees, "working for a real client, somebody who has commissioned the piece of work, will focus pupils' minds and provide an opportunity for them to develop presentation skills at the end of the project".

BIBLIOGRAPHY

1. Babbage, Charles (1832), <u>On the Economy of Machinery and Manufacturers,</u> Knight, London (in Images of Organisation, Morgan, 2006)

2. Beeden, Richard, (2008), <u>Times Education Supplement—TES Magazine</u>, 16 May 2008, P42

3. Browne, Ken, (2005), <u>Introduction to Sociology</u> (3rd Edition), Policy Press, UK

4. Brundrett, Mark, et al (2006), <u>Leadership in Education</u>, Sage Publications Ltd, London

5. Bush, Tony (2003), <u>Education Leadership and Management</u>, Sage Publication, London

6. Daft, Richard L, (2003), <u>Management,</u> 6th Edition, South Western

7. Fayol, Henry (1947), <u>General and Industrial Management</u>, Pitmans, London (in Images of Organisation, Morgan, 2006)

8. Huczynski, A. A. and Buchanan (2007), <u>Organisational Behaviour,</u> Pearson Education, Essex, England

9. Kamata, S (1983) <u>Japan in the Passing Lane</u>, Allen and Unwin, London (in Management Theories for Educational Change).

10. Kotter, J and Schlesinger, L (1979), <u>Harvard Business Review</u>, March 1979

11. Kurt, Lewin (1951), <u>Field Theory in Social Science:</u> Selected Theoretical Papers New York, Harper and Brothers.

12. Morgan, Gareth (2006), <u>Images of Organisation,</u> Sage Publications, Inc.

13. Morrison, Keith, (1998), <u>Management Theories for Educational Change,</u> Paul Chapman, London

14. Sepek, Jarek, (2008), <u>4YOUK Magazine</u> 3, June 2008, P12-13

15. Smith, Adam (1776), <u>Wealth of Nations,</u> Stratton & Cardell, London (in Images of Organisation, Morgan, 2006)

16. Taylor, G. R. (1979), <u>National History of the Mind,</u> Dutton, New York

17. Webber, Max (1947), <u>The Theory of Social and Economic Organisation</u>, Oxford University Press (in Images of Organisation, Morgan, 2006)

18. Whitehead, Stephen, (2005), <u>Management in Education Journal</u> [Vol. 19, Issue 3, 2005, P16]

MODULE TWO

Quality, Improvement And Effectiveness

Assignment Title:

In the light of issues discussed in this module and with reference to theoretical models presented in the literature, analyse and critically evaluate your own organization's strategies for educational improvement.

Included in your account should be a consideration of concepts such as effectiveness, accountability, quality and responsiveness.

To support your views you will need to access and examine relevant documentation from within your organisation, relating, for example, to aims, development, planning, monitoring and evaluation, performance tables, performance management, inspection reports, marketing.

(4,000-4,500 words)

A Brief Review and Critical Analysis of Issues in The Gambia's Post-Secondary Education System and Suggestions for Improvements in Quality and Effectiveness with reference to Institute of Professional Administration & Management IPAM (Gambia)

INTRODUCTION and PREFACE

As this assignment requires analysing and critically evaluating my own organisation strategies for educational development; I would like to focus on my previous work experience of both teaching and college management in an environment different from UK. I still hold consultancy clientele with the Institute of Commercial Management (ICM), a UK professional examining body based in Christchurch—Dorset (my roll there is to deliver contracts relating to marketing the institute programmes and assisting in developing educational institutions providing their courses in West Africa). Despite this connection, it could be difficult to complete this assignment focussing on ICM; for reasons such as inaccessibility to required documentation and reports. Having spent six years (1997-2004) in the past as the ICM Regional Co-ordinator for West Africa based in The Gambia, I was privileged to manage and develop a refugee educational project, The Institute of Professional Administration and Management (IPAM) where I was employed Principal and Director of Education (2000-2004).

Experience gained at IPAM opened to me, other areas of education research interests including *development of professional management in education, evaluation and assessment of qualifications, designing and recognition of distance learning qualifications, and effectiveness of vocational education projects in the rural areas of developing countries.* Let me please say at this point here that all information presented or disclosed in this paper is for academic exercise only and relating to meeting the requirements of this assignment.

The completion of this assignment therefore is based on experiences drawn on my work at IPAM (2000 and 2004) and during the period of which I was in charge of daily organisational operation of an educational institution that I developed from almost zero to recognition. This explains the management style of IPAM-before I joined the college, the changes I introduced when I took over and what I would like to recommend to my predecessor principal. Critical literature review covering other issues in education, particularly focusing on the UK system and relevant suggestions for improvement are included.

> "Education is the accumulation of knowledge, through learning, measured in standard, over a specific period of time"

Mohamed Sannoh, Keele University (2009)

THE PORTFOLIO OF THE MANAGEMENT OF IPAM (1998-1999)

The Gambia (most peaceful country in Africa)

Upon the outbreak of the civil war in the West African state of Sierra Leone in 1991 (1991-2000) many Sierra Leoneans sought refuge in The Gambia hence both countries have a lot in common such as the British colonial heritage and still maintain English language as their official language despite local tribal languages.

In addition, The Gambia is by far yet, at a competitive advantage of countries in Africa, being the most peaceful country on the whole continent under the present leadership of President Yahya Jammeh regardless of the local political debates and differences, although corruption is not one hundred percent free.

THE EFFECTS OF POLITICS ON EDUCATION IN AFRICA

Until recently, The Gambia had one radio station controlled by the state, no university and no television station.

> The Gambia now has a university—(The University of The Gambia or The UniGam)

One of the major credits accords President Yahya Jammeh even to the admiration of his opponents and critics, is the establishment of university in The Gambia through an extension programme with St. Mary's University in Halifax, Canada. Also, instead of sending Gambian children to secondary schools in Sierra Leone, President Jammeh's administration has ensured the establishment of many schools enabling access to educational foundation for every Gambian child and less expensive for their parents. Gambians can now have university education in their own country, although according to the late Professor Donald Ekon, Gambia University's first Vice Chancellor, during a conversation I had with him, most educators there require further studies and educational updates meaning that the new university's research and academic strengths were sill developing. I think Yahya Jammeh realised that the only way any leader can help his people is to develop them to achieve through education to acquire knowledge and live independently, a simple strategy that many African countries have not still took on board and that is why we are still backward; lack of education to enable us to think rationally. But Yahya Jammeh is now noted as the first African head of state to take the plunge and flush the mess to allow clean breathing air. He has a big heart for Africa and he needs special assistants to help him manage his heart.

In my own native Sierra Leone, it's a pity. The current All People Congress (APC) government under the leadership of Ernest Bai

Koroma has turned its back on education and educational values. The administration has so seriously undermined educational promotion that it can hardly be picked up in centuries to come even when they leave office. The APC administration, under Earnest Bai Koroma, has resulted in getting teachers to be come so deluded to the point of not having the ability to even live in good houses. In making ends meet, teachers have embarked on publishing and selling pamphlets in their subjects and the students bear the grunts of this commercial practice, because those who do not buy their teachers pamphlets will not pass exams, regardless of having the examiners prescribed and approved texts.

During the last Sierra Leone Peoples (SLPP) government under the leadership of President Ahmed Tejan Kabbah, educational promotion became highest on government's agenda to the extent that all examination fees of "Basic Education Certificate Examination (BECE) and Senior Secondary School Certificate Examinations (SSSCE)" conducted by the West African Examinations Council (WAEC) became free for all school children.

This promotion indeed gave birth to children of low income family background, the opportunities to work hard and enter higher institutions to qualify, get jobs and evade fundamental poverties they inherited at birth. Parents of large families with low income brackets who could not afford schooling sponsorships for all of their children welcomed the venture beyond political likeness but like "manna's from heaven", a complete God's gift. Just to be surprised that one of the first things on Ernest's agenda whose party they voted in office in the 2007 general and presidential elections was to eradicate this package and leave all educational expenses in the hands of parents to bear the responsibilities as he himself claims has never got free examination for his education in the past. At the same time, Ernest Bai Koroma's own biological two daughters Alice Koroma, born in Freetown and Danke Koroma born in London during the time his wife, Sia Nyama was studying psychiatric nursing in that country, occupies one of the most expensive houses in St. John's Wood in the city of London, again one of the most expensive cities in the world and are benefiting from free schooling (no fees paid) under the sponsorship of British government. Our first lady of Sierra Leone visits London every fortnight for shopping at Oxford Street fashion stores and at various shopping centres of Tesco and Safeway for their household daily feeding when she no longer works in Britain again and at the same time, the poor taxpayers of the country stays at home to haggle for "mina and bonga" heads at Krootown road market.

At the same time, Ernest Koroma's propaganda goes as far as publishing the following provocative comments on website for the world's attention:

> Take it or leave it, whatever shortcomings critics attribute to President Ernest Koroma's no-nonsense and uncompromising stand against corruption in Sierra Leone, one fact stands for sure—when the contemporary history of Sierra Leone is written, the President will certainly occupy an enviable place in Sierra Leone's folklore. He will forever be known as the first President of Sierra Leone who took a drastic stand against corruption, the seemingly impregnable beast that has wreaked untold havoc on socio-economic and political prosperity in our land.

My question again is where is this money coming from when the people in war stricken Sierra Leone are struggling hard to send their children to school to educate and benefit the country later? Is there anyway anyone can discuss education in Sierra Leone without addressing some of these facts and how they are affecting education in that country? Where do you think these people are heading for? Is it hell or heaven?

To everyone's surprised, we have never seen a ministry of education in the past in Sierra Leone that hates teachers like APC government Minister of Education, Minkailu Bah. Funnily enough, this young man, who also come the Northern Province of Sierra Leone, like Earnest Bai Koroma, was employed at Fourah Bay College working as a teacher and from there, he was appointed the Minister of Education. When Minkailu Bah wanted to express his disgust for teachers in the country, he called a press conference to comment on the government's motion to "revamp" education in the country and seized the opportunity to lambast teachers, by expressing the following, which got published in the internet for the attention of the world.

Minkailu Bah said in his press release that "while problems at home and in society contributed to poor performance, the **"generally negative attitude" of teachers bore the greatest responsibility"** when in fact he was saying that in capacity as APC government minister of education who has not paid loyal and devoting teachers serving the country for more than two years in some schools.

Is there any country in the whole world where teachers are meant to work voluntarily in their profession when the process of acquiring teaching qualification is very demanding, time consuming and expensive? How can they survive and look after their family if they are meant to work voluntarily? Was this the share of profits Earnest Bai Koroma promised the country in his presidential inauguration speech in the Siaka Stevens Stadium in 2007, that he is a businessman and he is going to run the country like a business organisation and declare profits to shareholders? Only "Sierra Leone Ltd." has this kind of business strategy that has not yet been discovered by professors at Keele University in UK.

If Minkailu Bah hates teachers so much and at the same time, he is the government minster of education, my question is *what is he doing*

in the ministry of education? This is just a clear indication of how politics affect the flow of education in Africa as clearly identified in the Sierra Leone and The Gambia Scenarios. In the case of Sierra Leone situation however, it is up to the voters to rectify their mistakes in the forth coming 2012 general and presidential elections.

While educational promotion is discouraged in Sierra Leone, there is now a state television in The Gambia and in addition to the radio station jointly called The Gambia Radio and Television Services (GRTS) and educational programmes are now highly encouraged on GRTS as president Jammeh's priority is heavily focused on education. And that is what I call government for the people and that is one of my areas of admiration of Yahya Jammeh of The Gambia.

The future effects of the scenario in these two countries is that there will be more educated of The Gambian population than that of Sierra Leone and for UK businesses in external education delivery such as the Institute of Commercial Management (ICM), Association of Business Executives (ABE) and external university education, there would be more market in The Gambia than in Sierra Leone because these are the population that are prepared and ready for post secondary education. That is good news for The Gambia and indeed, bad news for Sierra Leone because development in any country in the whole world starts with education and when a country, especially in Africa, is ignoring this fact, turning its back on educational promotion and developments as it is now happening in my native Sierra Leone, I'll begin to see what we are heading for. Sierra Leone no longer boasts of educational values as the "Athens of Africa", where the first higher educational institution of higher learning (Fourah Bay College) was founded. That is absolutely driving me mad!

Majority of Sierra Leoneans who arrived in The Gambia at the outbreak of the civil war in Sierra Leone were students, the educated graduate teachers, (such as now Hon. Shiaka Musa Sama of the PMDC) as well as university professors and other levels of practicing technocrats including chartered accountants, medical doctors, civil engineers, military personnel, politicians including John Benjamin, Chairman of the Sierra Leone Peoples Party and so on. The students included those in primary and secondary schools as well as post-secondary (following different technical and university education programmes) in Fourah Bay College, Milton Margai College of Education, Njala University College, Government Trade Centre, Freetown, Bunumbu Teachers Training College, Technical Institute, Kenema and so on.

There is no free schooling in most African countries including The Gambia. The United Nations High Commission for Refugees (UNHCR) attempted to cater for the educational needs of refugees in The Gambia including those from Sierra Leone, Liberia, Democratic Republic of Congo, Rwanda and Kassamance in nearby Senegal through the UNHCR regional office in Dakar; annexed in Banjul. That is why Yahya Jammeh is not only the president of The Gambia but the president of Africa.

A Gambian retired police commissioner, with no experience in handling refugee matters headed this office possibly, through his tribal or political connections in high places within the corridors of political powers in government. The UNHCR educational support, as said by the Gambia annex, was for schoolchildren (primary and secondary) attending Gambian government (not private or independent) approved schools, [even though such institutions have earlier on met the government conditions to operate and has been operating successfully]. Some parents still had to pay fees and other educational expenses for their refugee children attending schools in The Gambia.

This conditionality automatically excluded postsecondary students (such as IPAM students) from the UNHCR educational supports despite the fact that they were still genuine refugees and this discriminatory condition among others, brought some Sierra Leonean refugees together in 1999.

A Sierra Leonean by the name of Mr. Bangali, Information Technology consultant at Medical Research Council (MRC-Gambia) spearheaded the initiatives of the establishment of Institute of Professional Administration and Management (IPAM) in The Gambia and provided initial funding to cover purchase of furniture and payment of rent. He further donated some second hand computers to the institution to commence training for Sierra Leonean refugees at low cost fees of D2,000.00 (£50.00) per term (D6,000.00-£150.00) per year (according to the local currency exchange rate against the pound sterling at the time). That later proved to be high cost for many refugees who even had problems with meeting cost of daily adequate meals. However, this was not recognised until I took over the administration.

There was no formidable curriculum and the caretaker head (who eventually claimed ownership of the institution from Mr. Bangali) was a displaced student from a local business college in Freetown and with no experience in school management, seeking refuge in The Gambia. He relied heavily on inviting voluntary guest speakers from the business community including insurance salesmen, local traders, bank clerks and sometimes Sierra Leonean refugee teachers.

Training at IPAM at that time had no specific start and ending time as the principal who was also 'totally broke' was just interested in registering students and collecting whatever amount of money for fees. The secretary was not paid for eight months and instead, she was given hand out of about D20.00 (less than £1.00) per day to buy food and soft drinks. In June 1999, the principal travelled, through probably, the refugee resettlement programme to the United States of America

(USA). Before he left in that year, I was approached to manage the institution and appointed Principal and Director of Education.

I accepted the offer because it gave me *the opportunity to establish another market for ICM whose main business interest I was representing in The Gambia at the time and providing me with the privilege to manage a college especially in a special difficult circumstance.*

THE PORTFOLIO OF THE MANAGEMENT OF IPAM PART-2 (2000-2004)

When I took over the institution in 2000, I immediately applied for ICM approved centre status for official recognition as a teaching and examination centre under my supervision. According to ICM regulation for approve centre status, all colleges must be registered and approved by the Ministry of Education or Department of State for Education-DES(Education) in their own countries, where they exist. As IPAM was already an approved institution by the Department of State for Education of the Republic of The Gambia, this requirement was already in place. I used the DES (Education) college approval letter to apply to ICM in UK and this enabled ICM to take the application seriously.

Upon receipt of the ICM approval, I revisited the tuition fees previously charged and developed a new pricing strategy that focused on attracting more students with the ability to pay fees, hence the college solely relied on students fees.

As the education, market in The Gambia, by then was very highly price-sensitive and taking into consideration the exchange rate of conversion of the local currency (Dalasi) to pay registration and examination fees to ICM in UK, I thought of applying *"market penetration" pricing strategy* which Kotler (1994) explains as *the one that attracts more customers to a product or service in a market that is highly price sensitive.*

Instead of charging £50.00 per term (£150 per year), I reduced the fees to £50.00 per year and established a £100 part scholarship programme I advertised in the paper along side with the ICM approve centre certificate, for ICM courses about to start at IPAM for the June 2000 examinations. The £100.00 difference, which was part of the scholarship offer, became very attract to refugees as well as large members of The Gambian communities who were not refugees.

We attracted 500 applications within two weeks for sitting accommodation of 40 students at a time. We enrolled 120 students with good academic secondary school foundation including 50 Gambian nationals (who were not refugees) wanting to benefit from the indiscriminate IPAM low fees scheme.

I was able to run the college successfully until 2004 when I had to leave to join my family back UK, hence I was not able to implement other development strategies relating to quality, improvement and effectiveness. This is now discussed at this point as it may apply to the development of IPAM in The Gambia.

In addition, different relevant theories and concepts are explored and referenced to substantiate the suggestions and arguments and upon which they are based.

In a small institution like IPAM (Gambia), both leadership and management role rests on the shoulder of one person in the personality of the principal who sets and controls strategic direction of the institution's vision but without the support of effective management team (composed of his staff, teaching and otherwise), success is always disturbed, delayed or even undermined. In theory, IPAM should look at its strength, weaknesses, opportunities and threats (SWOT-analysis) to be able to plan strategically and move forward, but because the current situations there are unknown to me, it is impossible for me to produce such information in this assignment.

Accountability: It has been very difficult to provide a unique definition of accountability as it may refer to education according to Epstein (1993). Education workers are controlled by accountability to the market, authorities and other hierarchical lines of accountability that controls "ordinary" education workers.

The market accountability operates within a market or quasi-market situation and encourages the survival of organisations through fulfilment of contracts to provide services (or co-ordinates direct provision by others) for consumers. There is also political accountability facing educational institutions. Those who act on behalf of the electorate (whether elected representatives or paid officials) employ particular processes through which they hold themselves accountable for their stewardship.

Both market and political accountability groupings can be jointly subdivided under two further headings. Market constantly may stress on "accountability through service provisions or accountability through effective financial management". Accountability through service provision may refer to the organisation's responsiveness to consumer demands and ability to adapt its services accordingly.

However, accountability through effective management is not heavily stressed on the services themselves but the process by which they are provided. This may mean a stronger emphasis on the privatisation or contracting out of services if such moves will result in more efficient or effective financial management.

With political accountability, it could be accountability through elected representatives (local and national government). As strong advocates of increased citizen participation in the power of governance, there are, strong arguments that the electoral process alone is blunt a tool to achieve a fully participative democracy, as it renders citizens passive between elections.

A proposition for a more direct link between officers and councillors and the electorate as a form of "outward accountability" has been put forward in the process of developments. Another interesting concept presented by Hirch (1994) known as 'double democratisation' requires extending democracy 'downwards' (to the electorates) as well as 'upwards' (to the electoral representatives).

The current principal and staff of IPAM are controlled by the student market of The Gambia. They are bound to convince the market that students get value for money when they enrol there for studies and especially taking into consideration that there are many tertiary institutions now coming up in the country offering the same or similar services to the same target student market.

Now the general points as a simple means of reality within the student market responsible for the attractiveness of the market heavily depends on local knowledge understanding, published examination results (usually within league tables) and OfSTED inspection reports. Therefore, the quality of what is on offer has become inextricably linked to the ability of the organisation to maintain its ability to market its services.

They are also accountable to the government body of National Training Authority (NTA), assumed to be the (UK's OfSTED version of The Gambia) who oversees the operation of all tertiary institutions in the country. The regulation is that all institutions in this sector of educational provision must register with the NTA and pay registration fees. Thereafter, the registered institutions are charged, again to pay inspection fees (different from registration fees).

Upon their inspection, NTA may come up with their inspection reports requiring the institutions to provide certain amenities that may require the institution to spend even more money than what they have already spent on registration and inspection before granting approval and thereafter, the NTA asks the approved institutions to pay what they call annual fees, when The Gambian government have already stated that educational institutions are not taxable to run because it is the priority of the government to encourage the development of education as widely as possible so that many choices are opened to Gambian nationals in the country. Small tertiary institutions were flourishing and spinning up in different areas, but most of these were owned and managed by foreign nationals. Quickly enough, The Gambian authorities miscalculated that these foreigners are making enough money out of these education businesses we must establish a system of taxing them. Thereafter, the NTA was established to hammer out tertiary institutions under foreign ownership.

Within a short space of time, many institutions were short down for no good reasons, leaving their own Gambian nationals with uncompleted courses. What this so called government authorities failed to recognised was that these institutions were established in The Gambia and benefiting, in majority, Gambian nationals in particular. Taking such draconian measure against the institutions was uncalled for.

It is worth noting that payments of annual fees were continuous and is on the increase every year and existing institutions who do not meet any of the conditions are closed down and those planning to establish are not allowed to open doors.

The major difficulty private institutions in the vocational education sector are faced with, in The Gambia is that upon payment of these expenses, how much amount of money do institutions charge for fees from students to enable them operate conveniently (pay rents, pay teachers and buy materials) to enable quality provision of educational services? Interestingly enough, government (NTA) approval of a private institution attracts no financial assistance from government funding.

The NTA's powers are also extended to freezing vocational institutions bank accounts at will, in the process of enquiring the source of money the account holds. This means that even when an institution gets money from an outside donor paid directly into their bank accounts, such are liable to declaration to the NTA and accounted for its expenditure.

In the interest of accountability, again, one may like to know whether NTA are accountable to the Department of State for Education—DES (Education) for the money they collect from private tertiary institutions around the country and in the public interest of accountability, a blueprint to show how these monies are spent. The one million dollar answer every one is eager to know is this: *Who audits NTA and to whom are they answerable? To the president's office or to the office of the Department of State for Education? How much money have they collected from the private colleges so far? Can they publish this figure and how they are spent for the view of the public?*

THE ROLE OF MARKETING IN IMPROVING QUALITY OF IPAM's EDUCATIONAL PROVISION.

In his Marketing Education, Gray (1991) explains why educational organisations are concerned about marketing. From the Chartered Institute of Marketing's definition of marketing:

"A management process responsible for anticipating, identifying, and satisfying customer (consumer) wants and needs (requirements) with a view of making profit", means that every business involves in the practice or application of marketing is targeting profits as the end result benefits. Is it ethical for educational institutions to engage into the practice of marketing to generate profits for themselves? Why do educational institutions engage in marketing themselves?

According to Gray (1991), the major purpose of marketing in education "is to improve educational provision and practice in the belief that where marketing becomes integrated as a central aspect of school and college management, the other elements of management are improved. In turn, this will improve the range and quality of the institution's educational provision".

As marketing activities do not only start and ends with advertising or other elements of promotional activities the achievement of marketing which is "profit" does not only refer to excess of income over expenditure (which accountants call Credit Balance sheet). Profit in public sector organisations such schools and colleges, especially those that are government sponsored, mainly refers to the benefits the institution generates for those associated with it.

Management decisions referring to the investment of resources in these institutions is heavily dependent on the anticipated benefits if it yields to its direct immediate customers who are in this case the pupils and students. According to the concept relating marketing philosophy, manufacturers or producers do not only make what they want. They always find out first; what their potential customers actually want how they want, when they want it, where they want it and why they want it. There are also a series of legal, climatic, socio/cultural and so on, considerations to take into account.

All ideas about the product or service are researched first, and brought into the manufacturing or producing organisation. (The Outside-In-Perspective), according to Kotler, (1994). This gives the producers a though understanding that when the finished products or services are presented to the potential customers, they will be ready to buy; because they are presented with what they want or are expecting exactly (even though there could be existing competitive products or services). The reason for marketing philosophy or concepts is applied in this method is simply because the manufacturers are not producing for their own usage and satisfaction but for the satisfaction or benefits of their customers, who in this case, are the students as it may refer to educational institutions.

In education business, the institutions providing the services are bound to listen carefully to their students and their sponsors (customers) as this lays foundation of the careful examination of the need of customers they seek to satisfy and this would further empower them to stay in business.

Education providers like IPAM at tertiary post secondary level should understand that they are dealing with matured customers and most of these are very highly sensitive with what goes on the classroom and the educational institutions in general. They and their direct representatives or sponsors should be listened to very carefully. This close and constant links between educational institutions and their students (including sponsors) enable the institutions to be able to determine how they can improve on the quality of services they provide and this usually results in developing more structural and carefully planned strategies for their marketing services.

According to marketing terminology, consumers are those who use or eat the actual products or services. In most cases, another person who is referred to as the buyer pays for, the price. The buyers become customers when they buy from you more than once and frequently.

In education business, most of the people especially when they are very young that consumes the educational products or services are not buyers because they have no decision over the purchases. They are brought to school by their parents and pay their fees as the case may be in independent institutions (private schools). In government sponsored school (in UK), the fees and expenses towards education provisions form part of the social services the government provides. So, parents take the onus to bring heir children in local schools and have them registered for education.

Parent always want the best for their children and they believe that sometimes, particular schools can make a great difference in the life of children. The life chances of children as most parents believe, depends on the effectiveness of schools they attend according to MacBeath and Mortimore (2001).

Their research findings further says that children experience schools differently and that achievement is not a simple linear progression but subject to ebbs and flows over time and in response to the influence of the peer group and pupils own expectation on the basis of gender, race and social class. Additionally, schools as organisation may add value to that of its individual members or, on the other hand, may subtracts value and thereby enhancing and multiplying the skills of its members for their mutual growth.

Creative education also adds quality to learning institutions, which as Payne (1958) explains, places importance on a two-way traffic communication between the child and the teacher. *This art of control allows the child to discover, for him or herself rather than all the time, the child is spoon-fed with information.* The importance of creative education, is that it considers the child individually, creating every child into free, happy and able man and woman rather than considering their physiological and psychological make-up.

Situations in educational institutions, however becomes more complex the older the learner (students) becomes. In those earlier years, the parents had greater hands in deciding which educational institution the child goes. At the time the child gets ready to enter secondary school at the age of 11-12 years, the students have greater saying in deciding which secondary school they wish to attend and the trend continues, which may even dictate what they want to study, when they are ready to enter college or university. No doubt therefore, marketing at these post-secondary institutions are more directly focused on the students themselves.

Visibility through intangibility:

Some the major complexities of education marketing are that 'education is a service product'. It is intangible, meaning it cannot be seen with the naked eyes, physically felt and smelt. The quality of the very qualifications the educational provision leads to has to be anticipated by buyers as of quality before, during and after its provision. Secondly, the other fact about service sector provision is that both the producer and the consumer are together present during productivity.

As the buyer (customer/consumer) and the producer take part simultaneously in the production and consumption activities, the buyer immediately takes note of or experiences any mistake that occurs during the production activities,. If the mistake is very serious, it destroys the buyer's hope, which may even be resulted into driving the buyer away, and preventing other buyers from coming. Therefore, the producers of educational services must be very ready and thoroughly knowledgeable and versatile in what they produce to boost more confidence in buyers that they get value for money and where they are able to achieve this, the existing customers become 'free salesmen' through word of mouth recommendations to potential customers on behalf of the institution.

The strive for customer in education business to have this feel good factor usually result in quality perception and provision. Quality education is what every educational institution (schools, colleges and universities) all over the world communicates to its potential customers (potential students, parents and sponsors). What then is quality? What is a quality educational institution? Quality as a whole, as John Oakland (2008) explains, has never been able to provide a straightforward meaning because it is always subjective to the satisfaction of individual requirements. Quality signifies excellence of a product or service that all producers fight to achieve and it is only the customers and consumers can determine the level of quality after having experience of the service provision.

Tthe recognition and ease of an educational qualification and its utilisation particularly in the job market heavily determines the institutions quality. In The Gambia, qualifications from the IPAM institution at that time carry high level of respect among employers. During my service as a principal, company work placement experience, was introduced as a separate package to meet additional requirement the internal qualification the institute awarded under my signature. This provided a gateway to rapid employment facilities locally in the country, especially in the tourism sector. Those who were not able to pay external examination fees for ICM qualifications from UK went away with IPAM qualifications that put them in employment that fetched "bread and butter" on their breakfast tables.

A strong recommendation for a continuation of this system is suggested to cement efficiency, quality and improvement. Another incidence that actually puts more value on IPAM's qualification was the institution's graduation ceremony held in December 2002 at the exclusive Kairaba Hotel and which was attended by the then Secretary of State for Education, Ann Therese Ndong Jatta, who represented the President.

That was the first laudable graduation ceremony held at The Gambia by a tertiary institution that was not a university and it paid off a lot. Thereafter, I was given a contract to be part of the team and to design the graduation regalia of the University of The Gambia which they still use, including President Yahya Jammeh, the Chancellor of the UniGam. No wonder, the following intake, IPAM got full and went out of space for admission, not only for ICM courses, but IPAM qualifications.

In the event of achieving this element of marketing activities, "Total Quality Management" TQM has now become an important module in most courses relating to management and to further boost the awareness of Customer Care and Satisfaction. Like any other service provision business, educational service is also highly perishable.

Where for example, a school makes provision to hold 20 students in a class, the overhead cost of production remains the same even if there are only 5 students in the class within specific term of education.

For a better understanding, this can be presented mathematically as follows:

Cost of classroom per term = £300.00

Cost of tuition fess charged per student per term = £500.00

Number of students expected according to provision of places per term = 20 students

Amount expected (from 20 students) per term = £500.00 X 20 students=£10,000.00 per term.

Number of students turned up and paid £500.00 = 5students X £500=2,500.00

Cost of perishable services is therefore calculated as = £10,000.00-2,500.00=7,500.00

The above indicates that whether the school was able to get 20 students as anticipated or not the cost of production is unchangeable. Where the school has established quality status already, such high level of perish-ability could not have happened.

Quality of an institution in educational provision depends heavily on:

 i. the quality of the teachers/lecturers (their qualifications and experience and exposure)
 ii. library resources (availability of enough educational materials relating to courses offered)
 iii. location of the institution (whether is is located in a learning environment or distractive location where learning is constantly disturbed by factory noises)
 iv. administration of the institution (referring to how courses are organised, progress monitored and recorded with certainty consistently).

IPAM should therefore endeavour to continuously employ well-qualified lecturers in their different areas of learning or where there are lacks, makes provisions for different forms of staff trainings and developments programmes.

The institutions heavily depend on extra resources coming in, this is achievable by addressing the question of quality adequately, and another aspect of education marketing is that there is no specific blueprint design activity to follow. The effectiveness of the results achievable depends on many factors but heavily on the personnel designing the marketing efforts and the realities the marketing message sends out.

"In-house marketing" within educational institutions can play high value on quality of the institution. Within the institution itself, staffs have to be aware of the kind of business in which they are and be ready and able to identify their immediate customers (within the organisation) and know how to satisfy them. They work in-group and aim at producing high quality jointly pulling in the same direction for total benefits of the organisation.

As price competition is not allowed in education business (at least in UK), it is sometimes difficult or almost impossible to differentiate quality institutions based on price. Like other service delivery organisations, educational institutions differentiate their services image basing on three main areas including: people, physical environment and process. Institutions are building brand image and status-quo symbols to differentiate them from others in order to gain completive advantage edge over others in the same business.

Private post-secondary institutions such as the IPAM (Gambia) are different in that they heavily depend on applications common with any other ordinary services providing business enterprise because they rely solely on student fees as main source of income and receive no financial supports from government.

In the last ten years, the British education system has experienced some changes. First, the shifting of control from the education providers (institutions, teachers, local authorities and professional bodies) to consumers (parents and employers and communities) with the government's main objective of creating high level of competition to increase the standard in productivity according to the 1988 Education Reform Act.

However, the main benefit this has produced is reduction in public expenditure and waste; thus creating 'value for money'.

Now public sector education is experiencing market economy. City Technology Colleges and Grant Maintained Schools both funded by the Department of Education and Science (DES) are now co-existing in UK.

Further to this, the proliferation of private training organisations has raised new dimension of competition among post-secondary education sectors, being intensified by the privatisation of part of Training Agency and its Skills Training Agency funded by government and runs within business philosophy by business people. This new agenda is heavily focused on vocational training.

Since the 1970s, the UK education system, coupled with the reduction of students population has experienced a network of a series of competition and changes forcing some government sponsored schools to 'opt out' of local authority control. This is a way of preventing closure due to high competition, which the market forces have presented to educational institutions.

The 1986 Education Act has placed more responsibilities on institutions within the post-secondary sector. Such responsibilities have emerged with the call of Annual Parents' Meetings at which governing bodies must report on and justify school policies and plans.

During such meetings, parents have the opportunity to pass resolution to be heeded by governing bodies and membership has been manipulated to increase further responsibilities. Definitely in the post-secondary education sector, there is now voice power, stronger than ever being further supported by consumerist voice institutions such as Advisory Centre for Education (ACE), National Association for Governors and Managers (NAGM), National Union of Students (NUS).

BIBLIOGRAPHY

1. David, Russell and Patel, Ashok De Montfort University, Leicester: Cost Management: an introduction to Japanese management practice (August 1999 p2 issue of ACCA Students' Newslettert

2. Glover and Paul Thomas-EDU-40002, Developing Education Management Series, Keele University

3. Gray, J. (1990) "The Quality of schooloing: frameworks for judgements" British Journal of Education Studies. Vol. 38, No. 3, 1990

4. Hirsch, D (1994) A Positive Role for Local Government Lessons for Britains from Other Countries London, LGC Communications.

5. Howard Gardiner, (1983) Frames of Mind, New York, NY Basic Books

6. Imai, Masaaki (1986) The Key to Competitive Success, Random House

7. John Macbeath and Peter Motimore (2001) Improving School Effectiveness, Open University Press

8. John S. Oakland (2008), TQM Butterworth, Heineman

9. Kent, Reuben, Crissis in he Classrooms: Shepherd's Bush Gazette, P1 November 14, 2008

10. Kogan, M. (1997) Education Accountability: An analytical overview, Hutchinson, London

11. Kotler, Philip, (1994) Marketing Management: (analysis, planning and implementation) Prentice Hall

12. Macbeath, J. (el al) (2006) Leadership for Learning, University of Cambridge

13. M. A. Payne (1958), Creative Education, William Macmillan

14. Sensenbrenner, Joseph, (March/April, 1991 vol. 69, issue 2 p 64-75-Harvard Business Review), Quality Comes to City Hall

MODULE THREE

Strategic Management In Education

Assignment Title:

Outline and critically evaluate to theory, the process of strategic management in the development of a plan in your working scheme.

(3,000-3,500 words)

An outline and critical evaluation of the development of an effective Vocational Business Studies programme designed for meeting the demands of employers in profit and non-profit making organisations.

Preface and Introduction:

This paper aims at producing the facts that there have been and will always be some amount of criticisms about existing provisions for Business Studies programmes within the school curriculum or those of the various professional bodies and other training institutions including private colleges.

Due to the variety of criticisms from various quarters including government, employers within industries and business communities, educational institutions and students' as well, there is always a need for continuous improvements to review, revaluate, make relevant adjustments and to address issues of concern in order to meet requirements of stakeholders' satisfaction.

This is relevant because as the business communities are not stagnant and not universally the same, there are bound to be variations in needs for requirements in different environment which are all dictated by the topographies that are never controlled by unified distinctive factors. The paper further reveals that business practice is vocational and definitely demands practical requirements that are determined and driven by results achievement focus.

The training approach requires that focus on this fact should not be taken lightly during the training process of people who are expected to develop career in business activities if only the business studies programme is to become in anyway meaningful.

However, due to the environmental differences and conditions affecting business practices universally, it may not be possible to operate a single rubber stamped model. In this programme as well, the same principles apply but with the understanding that a unified requirement (building confidence, developing sense of responsibility as work culture and placing value on customers) are all taken into considerations seriously, no matter where the idea of business practice is applied.

According to the November 2008 reports of the International Financial Services London published by Financial Services Education & Training (page 1), the UK has a long tradition of supplying education and training services to international students and professionals.

The same report further highlighted the wide range of educational, occupational and other specialists training provision in the financial and services in the UK. The key providers mentioned in this report are professional institutions, pre-employment education services offered by universities, business schools and further education colleges; and other private sector suppliers such as the exchanges, specialist training firms and industry associations.

It is of the opinion that the Business Studies programme this paper addresses fulfils the employer requirements gap in the work place in commerce and industries although not, specifically in the financial services sector.

Why do educational institutions exist? Why do students enter institutions to study? Why do they choose their choice of areas of studies? Why do they choose their specific title of qualifications; being a certificate, diploma, degree, etc?

The answers to these questions vary from one person to another. For some, it is out of curiosity to know more, some are after the prestige of having letters after their names, and some seek specific employment, whilst others pursue promotions in their current employment. Some people enter institutions to study due to pressures from their parents and influence from friends or peers they admire and respect. Some choose particular areas of studies to carry on family line of business; some listened to teacher's advice from career counseling service in their schools and so on.

Whatever is the reason, the fact is that we all enter different educational institutions to learn. The next question is: what is learning? According to Pip Hardy, et al (1993) of University of Sunderland, "learning is a change in knowledge, skills and behaviour."

The authors went on to emphasise that learning process varies from being taught at lecture in the classroom but further went on to encompass other methods, by reading about it, by practicing to master the skills, by watching a demonstration, by becoming curious and participating though trials and errors and most commonly, by learning from mistakes.

In their joint presentation on Qualifications and Experience: What employers know and don't know about their workers' ability . . . , Fernando Galindo-Rueda and Romesh Vaitiligam (7 April 2003) of the London School of Economics stated that employers pay for workers ability as they get to know them better, but they don't pay for it as much as they should, especially for less educated workers.

Their study of wage inequality, demonstrates that qualifications are imperfect signals of individual skills and British employers rely less on them as indicators of productivity as they get to know their workers better.

However, relatively able but less educated workers appear to find it very difficult to advertise their skills to other potential employers, giving a strong bargaining power to their incumbent employers.

"Qualification credentials are intended to certify that an individual has acquired a determined level of skills. But they also reveal to employers a more general type of ability that has enabled individuals to learn and acquire a determined qualification—in other words, they have a strong informational value independently of their educational content. Statistical discrimination in favour of more educated individuals may occur when in the absence of better information, more educated individuals are known to be on average more productive than less educated ones" the report claims.

The report, which tests two hypotheses, identified the following further:

> *"1. Do employers discriminate between workers according to their schooling, but tend to rely less on qualifications as they learn more about their workers' ability?*

2. *Is there an 'insider informational advantage' for incumbent employers, which allows them to pay less for their workers' skills than they otherwise would?*

Empirical investigation of these hypotheses comes up with the following results:

i. *Individuals with higher ability experience faster wage growth as they accumulate experience. Ability is the individual characteristic that accounts for most of the wage growth experienced by workers.*

ii. *For a given experience level, increased time spent with the same firm makes schooling less valuable. For workers in manual occupations, ability becoming more valuable with higher tenure supports private learning by incumbent employers as opposed to widespread learning.*

iii. *As workers stay longer with the same firm, higher ability becomes a stronger indicator of the probability of receiving training. Firms thus appear to (a) screen workers in order to maximise their own net benefits of training; and (b) provide learning when they know that workers have a lot to lose if they decide to quit and move to another firm. This loss is particularly strong for blue-collar workers.*

The implication for government policy is clear. Less educated individuals who are more likely to focus on blue-collar occupations or choose a vocational route after leaving school need a reliable system of credentials.

Such a system must genuinely reflect excellence at the skills learned as well as proof of the capacity to learn more specific skills on the job. Even though there may be efficiency reasons to rely on firms to provide the full extent of vocational learning, over-reliance on them without addressing the problem of insider informational advantage will surely lead to increased bargaining power for employers with all benefits from learning accruing to the latter.

On a more general level, this research makes a strong case for simulating the impact of the introduction of new qualifications on a new dimension related to the way employers set their expectations about the ability of individuals with both old and new qualifications. Stigma effects can unexpectedly wipe out the informational value associated with certain credentials, with considerable loss to learners, employers and the wider society that subsidised such reforms".

The 17th Edition of the Key Note Market Report 2008 established that UK employers spent £20.98bn on off the shelf training during spring 2008 representing 3% increase on the previous year and the major proportion of this money is spent on internal training. The Kay Note further approximates that UK employers spend around £3.3bn on external trainers. Further to this estimate is that of the Learning and Skills Council's National Employer Skills Surveys report for 2008 estimated that employers in England spent £38.6bn on training in 2007.

As the UK training industry is enormous and incorporates an array of suppliers from the traditional training company to IT companies and professional associations thousands of small organisations, often family business organisations including sole traders are emerging to service the industry. The Commercial Management College being developed becomes part of this statistics in UK.

More companies are now becoming more specific about training benefits; that are specifically relevant to their firms. The Key Note Market Report 2008 further states that the Training Advisor at the Charted Institute of Personnel and Development (CIPD), Martyn

Sloman indicates that the use of coaching and in-house training is increasing as is e-learning and this may trigger training providers to redesign their programme to suit customer demands. Whether organisations are looking to maximise the benefits of training is another concern. Although, however, the majority of organisations continue to buy external training programmes, Learning and Development survey of the CIPD 2008 raised the alarm that significant proportion of employers either do not buy or have ceased to buy training from external providers which by no means should worry the training industry.

Pip Hardy, et al (1993) went on further to say that another major element that triggers learning is the idea of feeling good about something you do and enjoy. If people feel good about some thing they do and enjoy best, it is likely that the pleasure they get out of it encourages them to find out more and thereby causing them to learn more about it.

Different models of education exist and different educational institutions each have their own methods of educational delivery.

For example, many institutions deliver educational programmes within specifically designed syllabus within a prescribed period and thereafter, students' participants tested to prove their levels of understanding through some form of examination, usually written examinations to the satisfaction of the education designers or providers. Has this always been the most effective system of education?

If the course is designed just to provide a learning knowledge about, say the history of the past event; like the assassination of Julius Caesar, which requires no mastering of practical skills for working skills development purpose, then the exact explanation of what happened in the Roman senate on the day the Roman leader was killed would be enough.

If on the other hand, learning requirement expects the students' ability to practically build a house, sell a product, teaches a student, to bake a cake and so on, the knowledge requirements of such learning expects more than classroom expressions.

Here, the participating students only prove the learned skills by having the ability to practically engage in doing the trade well. Therefore, the historical knowledge of just knowing the past (which, basically is just theoretically academic) fall short of the requirements of the knowledge of knowing practically (which is more of a vocational input, having mastered the ability to perform a task practically well).

Tony Bush (2008) speaks lengthily about this in his Educational Leadership and Management and somehow finds it difficult to differentiate the importance of theory over practice and verse versa. Therefore, he referred to theory as systematic guide to practice although in the real world, most practitioners tend to be dismissive of theories and concepts for their alleged remoteness from the real situation.

Tony Bush further went on to state that theory is also unfashionable with policy-makers and government agency and then sited those such as English Office for Standards in Education (OFSTED) and the Teacher Training Agency (TTA).

In asserting support for Tony Bush, Willower (1980, p2) declared that 'the application theories by practising administrators is a difficult and problematic undertaking.' He further went on to clarify that theories cannot simply become useful very much in the realm of practice.

Among the list of other theory sceptics are Holmes and Wynne (1989 pp1-2) who are not too comfortable about the use of theory to inform practice clearly stated that: "there can be little genuine theory in educational administration.

It is an applied field ultimately dependent on human will acting within a social context . . . So it is unproductive to look for a set of theories . . . by which educational administrators may guide administrative behaviour".

Within the education providers sector in the UK, there has been too much of theoretical approach to education provisions and this approach has raised a series of concerned within the employers in commerce and industries as observed by Keith Morrison (1998). That the business community has already expressed their dissatisfaction through accusations that education standards have not measure up to their expectations because of producing illiterate, innumerate and work-shy employees who are totally not prepared to become useful for what they need.

This accusation by the business industries has brought in retaliation, a backlash accusation feedback by the education community.

According to Entwistle (1981), who confronted the employers that they have just unnecessarily become very difficult by turning the working environment into an uncomfortable atmosphere to the extend of turning the world of work into the graveyard of aspirations, creativity, flexibility, adaptability, breadth and problem solving—capabilities developed painstakingly by schools in their students. This statement also received supports from Simon and Taylor (1981).

Their argument of defence is hat education is not a tangible product that one can see. It cannot be bought, sold, and haggled about before buying as in the case of other tangible goods such as car or chair.

Also, education providers' ague that education is not producing a single product at a time in factory and that competition has no place in the provision of educational programmes in educational institutions. As schools are not production lines, students can therefore not be expected to be moulded as passive objects to be shaped into a specific object for a specific functional purpose.

Another advocate for education providers, Wilby (1997: 18) became explicitly adamant by stating that education would not introduce business practice because business organisations have less or no value for morals and also that they are undemocratic and self centred and focused only or mainly on their profits. Business ethics are distrustful of their partners and are all profits driven.

From the two sides' point of view, it is hard to judge who is wrong or right. From personal analysis point of view however, one can see that business community's points are well raised to reflect the fact they expect certain basics from fresh school leavers to be able to fit into the world of work easily and build on the skills gradually.

The expectation is therefore that schools should provide these basics in conjunction with what they want and that should be embedded into the school curriculum of provision. Should schools consider this appropriate and how should they go about doing this?

Do they need specific guidance from the business communities regarding their requirements? How would they go about developing this?

In the process of leadership and management practice, again, according to Tony Bush (2003) the art usually is, regarded as essentially practical. Therefore the practice of educational leadership and management is not an exception to this because the determination of vision, the allocation of resources and the evaluation of effectiveness are action required before they become meaningful. Tony Bush further says that academics develop and refine theory while managers engage in practice; bringing about the theory/practice divide or gap and this stands as the Gordian Knot of educational administration.

English (2002 pp1 and 3) says that the theory-practice gap has become a permanent fixture of landscape because it is embedded in the way we construct theories for use and that the gap will only be removed when we construct different and better theories that predict the effects of practice.

Although, however the implementation of Education Reforms Act (1988) and subsequent legislation in England and Wales have heavily emphasised on the effects of practice rather than theories on educational leadership and management, the importance of theories are seen by many as being most useful for influencing practice because they suggest new ways in which events and situations can be perceived.

Through empirical research, as suggested by Hughes and Bush (1991 p.234), fresh insight are eventually provided by focussing attention on possible interrelationships that the act of practice has not noticed. This creates room for further exploration and facts tested through empirical research. This may further reduce the theory-practice gap considerably where the result becomes a better understanding of practice. Therefore, theory cannot, totally be dismissed as being irrelevant to understanding educational programmes requiring practical functions. It is valuable and significant particularly in educational programmes if it serves to explain practice and provide educationists with action plan guides.

In their contribution to the effectiveness of practice, Copland et al.,(2002 p75) said that if practitioners shun theory, they must heavily rely on practical experience to guide and justify actions; meaning that at anytime decisions are needed to implements actions, decision makers always count on those with the relevant practical experience for advice.

However, experience alone as challenged by Leithwood et al (1999 p75) may not be very helpful as the sole guide to taking action especially when the decision maker begins to operate in different context and environment. As organisations are variable in different environments by nature, this may mean that the different variables dictate the action requirements. A broader knowledge and awareness of theories in educational leadership and management for example, is by no doubt valuable when the education manager (head teacher/principal/director of education) is faced with tasks to interpret and implement penalty for behaviour in different situation with different culture and methods of prevailing practice.

In Sierra Leone for example, girls are not allowed to wear hair extensions and neither are they allowed to go to school without having their hair plaited or else they are sent home.

They not allowed to wear jewelleries like rings, chains and drops earrings to school or else they are sized and returned to their parents only at the end of year PTA meetings.

Where as in UK, girls behaving in school environments in such manner may mean nothing or something else and may carry different penalty or nothing at all.

Another setback to decision making based on personal experience for interpreting facts is that it is practically narrow and discards heavily, the opinion and valuable knowledge of other team members. Secondly, rigorous exploration of theories usually emerges with developing models that helps to explain events and behaviour.

Understanding of this variety of theories would eventually help to avoid silly mistakes that usually occur in the process of acquiring practical experience.

As this paper caters to establish an outline and critical evaluation of the development of an effective Vocational Business Studies programme suitable for meeting the demands of employers in profit and non-profit making organisations, it is assumed that the current provisions have not gone far enough to meeting the industry demands. Therefore, this justifies and further requires the needs for change in the education provisions to serve the business community. This approach, like any other form of change, is being regarded as a dynamic and continuous process of development and growth that involves a reorganisation in response to felt needs, in this case of employers in commerce and industries.

According to Morrison's (1998) theory, it is a process of transformation, a flow from one state to another, initiated in this instance, by external forces (the employers in commerce and industries) involving the institutions leading to a realignment of existing values, practices and outcomes. This new provision is not considered the best and the last. It is an attempt to continuous improvement process, which Mintzberg (1987) agrees as pre-planned and an emergent open-ended approach.

Practically, in the process of approaching change, needs assessment/ analysis is an essential feature in commencing the planning of change. Therefore, we need to investigate what areas actually need change as preference as it may refer to any of such as discrepancy, want, deficit, desired as may be required. Knowledge of these may help planners to assess the size of the needs, the priorities for the needs, the number of people who are likely to be affected, the consequences for not meeting the needs, the needs are met, the resources and costs of meeting the needs and how to put the change of needs into operation.

STRATEGIES FOR DEVELOPMENT AND IMPLENTATION OF THE BUSINESS STUDIES PROGRAMME:

Where are we now with the level of employers' satisfaction of educational qualification relating to business studies programme?

In the process of developing strategies for the development of the new Business Studies programme this paper aims to achieve, current or prevailing issues affecting or disturbing employer satisfaction are identified first.

<u>This mainly is, there are too much of emphasis on theories placed on current programmes with little or no practical input, as priorities, before graduating.</u> This situation has resulted into the emergent of the following situations of facts:

i. Employers seem to believe that those graduating with academic qualifications are no doubt, learned theoretically but they are not very comfortable with their performance to a large extent because they are not quite sure whether they are prepared enough to immediately commence work practically, when it comes to practical realities in the work place. This means that most young graduates with academic qualifications leave their institutions unprepared to start work immediately as far as the employers are concerned.

ii. The employers are not interested in hiring those with academic papers or those with letters after their names from prestigious institution but more interested in hiring those with the ability, capability, the right attitude and willingness to perform work roles in the work place.

iii. Therefore, Educational institutions responsible for designing or delivering courses in preparation of people for work, must consider this idea if only they work in the interest of their students, the industries and societies they promise to serve.

Although there are many forms of strategy with different levels of interest to most managers, the strategy explored to apply in this project are simple and applicable to the point of achieving what the project is seeking. They are meant to be definitions of directions, which consistently concentrate on the pursuits of interest with rooms for flexibility should there be a need or a reason for change in the interest of achievement.

So where do we want to get to? In other words, what do we want to achieve? Focus on these questions would eventually address the Strategic Objective of the project. This will clearly spell out, as outline in our Mission Statement of the educational institution, The Commercial Management College. Therefore, all activities designed or scheduled in the interests of the project (the college) must have the focus in mind. According to Mintzberg (1987b) the strategy set must be for a reason because strategy management that just emerge without a reason has no purpose.

If we can revisit Druckers's idea according to Gordon Pearson (1999) on purposive issue, we can ask the questions:

1. *What business are we in?*
2. *Who are our customers?*
3. *What do they value?*

The answers are:

1. *We are in the business of designing and delivering educational programmes to provide knowledge in Business Studies.*
2. *Our customers are those who either want to acquire knowledge in the business disciplines and produce at high quality satisfactorily for their employers or establish self-business for*

themselves and become successful entrepreneurs. Our customers are, also extended to owners of established organisations seeking knowledgeable personnel to work for them; as well as to state governments who rely on knowledgeable personnel to ensure that the affairs of state including development or creation of industries are successful for the enhancement of creating employment in the country.

3. *They value the ability of having both academic and practical knowledge to equip them with the abilities to perform well on the job and to transfer their skills unto others, to facilitate appropriate technology. Therefore, all strategies on plan being it a long term or short term strategy must always focus on addressing issue of the questions and answers as stated.*

Mission Statement that defines the Strategic Objective.

The Commercial Management College

TRAINING PEOPLE TO GET JOBS AND PROMOTIONS
OR BECOME ENTREPRENEURS

We exist to train people to get jobs and promotions through a unique education that breaks the barrier of traditional academic system. We place more value on creating opportunities for gaining experience through apprenticeship during learning without undermining academic essence in education. We are able to achieve this mission by ensuring that before students graduate we assist them to:

- *communicate effectively*
- *solve problems confidently*
- *become self reliant*
- *get on with others professionally*
- *demonstrate good leadership*
- *respect the importance of customer care*

which are relevant requirements of employers in the business management sector as well as entrepreneurship.

Another point of consideration is on the different levels of milestones to explain how we can achieve the mission statement of the Commercial

Management College; which may focus on itemising our activities of successful operation that makes solid impact, different from the current educational deliveries focusing on business studies.

In the first place, we are designing this programme, not for our own personal satisfaction. We aim, through the college programmes of delivery, to satisfy target audience including:

1. Students, to ensure that they get both theoretical and practical knowledge before they graduate; in readiness for employment. Where they decide to embark on private business practice, they are equipped with confidence and balanced capability to become entrepreneurs.
2. Employers', to ensure that they employ a set of new young graduates of business studies qualifications who are fully equipped with the academic knowledge as well as practical experience. This prepares them fully to commence fulltime work with little instructions to the satisfaction of their employers.
3. The state in which the programme operates by delivering a system of education that caters for building the intelligence and confidence in young people that assist and contribute to the national interest of job creation in the country.

If we can go back to the introductory questions at the beginning of this paper:

Why do educational institutions exist? Why do students enter institutions to study? Why do they choose their choice of areas of studies?

Why do they choose their specific title of qualifications; being a certificate, diploma, degree, etc?, we will discover that there are many well-established educational institutions delivering courses for business studies qualifications of different identities from certificates to postgraduates, but are some of these actually qualifications or just prestigious letters after people's name? What is the point of having any qualification that cannot fetch employment or entrepreneurial capability that generates financial income to put bread and butter on your breakfast table?

At the Commercial Management College, courses are designed to deliver education internationally through partnerships with other institutions under strict rules and conditions, ensuring that practical approach through learning is sandwiched by relevant theories and as special modules in their own rights before certification.

This correspondence type of marketing strategy becomes suitable in reaching far to a large number of students' worldwide and further maintains quality on the College awards that graduates are both qualified and experienced to the delights of employers as well as guaranteeing entrepreneurship foundation skills for private business start-ups, the graduates can take advantage of.

Having considered the strategies of the major players in the education delivers' market, the next question to ask according to Kotler's (1994) marketing strategy is that the college further tries to differentiate itself from the norms of the strategic groups involved in marketing British qualifications, especially to overseas market.

That is why different methods of delivery are identified, as indicated in the programmes designed brochure, providing different choices for the convenience of students who are the main customers.

Conclusion:

The organisational culture at Commercial Management College focuses on pattern of students' development reflecting on learning process to understand the fact that different groups of people have different ways of life and values, unique in their own rights.

This understanding helps organisational leaders further to understand cross-national variations in organisation and target markets and thus serves as a major strategy to compete in the student market the Commercial Management College is entering.

Imparting this knowledge empowers students into future business leaders to focus on well-defined values, respect for the environment, and awareness of barriers leading to segregation, methods of production, management and delivery in specific manners that differentiate themselves from others. Our students' are our target customers and without them, we cannot exist. They always come first and that is why we always listen to them very carefully.

Please Note: The full design of the Commercial Management College for practical implementation is enclosed herewith in the Index for examiners perusal.

BIBLIOGRAPHY

1. Pip Hardy et al (1993) Effective Learning. Learning Development Services, University of Sunderland

2. Bush, T. (2008) Theories of Educational Leadership and Management Paul Chapman Publishing Ltd. London

3. Willover, D.J (1980) Contemporary Issues in Theory in Educational Administration. Educational Administration Quarterly 16(3): 1-25

4. Holms, M and Wynne E. (1989) Marketing the School on Effective Community: Belief Practice and Theory in School Administration, Lewes Falmer Press

5. Entwistle, H (1981) Work, Leisure and Lifestyles, Batsford, London

6. Simon, B. and Taylor, W. (1981) Education in the Eighties, Batsford, London

7. Wilby, P. (1997) Business Doesn't Means Best When it Comes to Schools. The Times Education Supplement December 12-18.

8. English, F. (2002) Cutting the Guardian Knot of Educational Administration: the theory practice gap. The Review 44 (1): 1-3.

9. Hughes, M. And Bush, T (1991, P. 234) "Theory and Research as Catalyst for Change" Advancing Education: School Leadership in Action, London Falmer Press

10. Copland, et al (2002, p. 75) Leadership Teaching and Learning: A Framework for Research and Action. Pril, New Orleans

11. K. Lieithwood et al (1999, p75) Changing Leadership for Changing Times. Open University Press, Buckingham.

12. Morrison, K. (1998) Management Theories for Educational Change, Paul Chapman Publishing Co. London

13. Mintzberg, H.(1987), Crafting Strategy. Harvard Business Review, March/April 66(2) 66-75

14. Mintzberg, H. (1987b), The Strategy Concept (ii): Another Look at Why Organisations need Strategies. California Management Review, USA

15. Pearson, G. (1999) Strategy in Action, Pearson Education Limited, UK

16. International Financial Services London (IFSL) Research of Financial Services Education & Training, November 2008.

17. Key Note Market Report (17th Edition, November 2008) Edited by Katie Hughes ISBN: 978-1-84729392-3.

18. Kotler, P. (1994), Marketing: (Analysis, Planning, Implementation and Control) Eith Edition. Paramount Communications Company, Englewood Cliffs, New Jersey 07632, USA.

MODULE FOUR

Resource Management In Education

Assignment Title:

It has been argued that over the last two decades education has been re-structured by the introduction of market competition. Discuss this phenomenon and its impact on resource management in your organisation (or in an organisation known to you).

Upon successful completion of this module you will have successfully;

   a.   Demonstrated a broad understanding of significance of global economic issues on local resource availability, allocation and management.
   b.   Understood the concept of marketisation of education
   c.   Related these concepts to issues of resource availability, allocation and management to your own organisation or organisation known to you.

(Approximately: 3,000 words)

INFLUENCE OF MARKET COMPETITION ON RESOURCE MANAGEMENT IN EDUCATION

Preface

Resource management is one of the most important tools of management of any organisation. Again, the effectiveness of resource management determines the extent of the success or failures of the organisation. As Galick and Urwick (1973), refer to management as the process of getting activities completed efficiently and effectively with and through other people, other writers have further extended to say that other factors in addition to other people includes materials and finances.

This presentation has looked into the different systems of state economies known as markets such as socialism (state controlled) communist as well as the free market systems as practiced by different countries around the world. Also the benefits of free market systems as compared to others are identified.

Introduction to market:

Market is generally referred to as a place where buyers and sellers meet to exchange goods and services with the products worth determined by the agreed price payable in acceptable money currency. In most markets now-a-days, there is no one supplier of a product or service; so there is no one buyer of the product or service in the same market; meaning that where in any market, many buyers and many sellers exist, it is practical for the market to become competitive especially for the sellers.

The fundamental studies of economic practice relating to facilitating the achievement of profit depends on the law of demand and supply: *'the lower the price, the higher the quantity of demand and the higher the price, the lower the quantity demanded'* assuming that other factors influencing demand remain constant (ceteris paribus).

When however, the supply and demand activities reach at a point where the price at which the quantity demanded equals the quantity supplied in the market, (the demand and supply curves overlaps), it is known as the equilibrium price point, meaning that no loss or profit occurred here.

As the main objective of firms assumed by economists is to maximize profits, competition drives firms to put more efforts in the design and production of their products and services to attract more buyers to them than to their competitors; within the legal framework of marketing practice.

Profit is referred to as the difference between Total Revenue and Total Cost (TR-TC=Profit). If a firm, for example, receives £1,000,000TR from selling its output and spends £900,000TC producing this output, its profit is £100,000P. Within the same theory of profit maximization, government and like minded funders of projects consider allocation of resources to organisations according to justification of their activities; to avoid waste of limited resources.

Central control system (Communism):

Communism or totalitarian system is practical with countries of central controlled plan system of government, as it was recently in the then USSR member states like Russia and also the UK during the Second World War (where even food was rationed to the public under strict control system). In this system, it is the central state agency that decides what should be produced for the benefits of the population focusing on the provision of the human basic rights such as health, education, protection, etc.

When the document of fundamental rights of citizens in England was published Adam Smith (1776), it was discovered that a major section of these rights was the right of free access to education, which was a part of cooperative efforts to enhance national developments rather than basically individuals. Other state ideas started emerging within the framework of cooperative efforts around other activities that people could agree to better achieve collectively, rather than singularly. These were often services that, by their implementation, would benefit the public at large and retained the original spirit of the state as a cooperative effort of individuals to better achieve their idea of the good life.

This was the emergence of socialist ideas in Britain encouraged by the citizens; a system that controls state resources for "fare share for all". The same system also applied to the provision of education for all in UK.

Socialism or totalitarian is different from the free market economy system *where resources are allocated according to the operation of the market as dictated by the forces of demand and supply pulls.* There are instances where certain organisations do not perform as efficiently as expected, causing their performance to fall below expectation known as market failure.

Where governments are responsible for allocation of resources they are justified to interfere in the market mechanism as one of the steps for improves and agency accountability to the central government.

Free market economy is also characterised by free trade without any tariffs or subsidies imposed by the government. The role of the government in a country that practice free market economy is only limited to controlling the law and order to ensure that qualifies fair trading system.

In reality, the basic feature of the free market economy is that only people with sufficient control over resources, and wealth, in particular have the privilege to purchase goods and services, often priced very highly in a free economy. Prices, which are the only allocating and distributing factor in a free market economy, place the poor in an unenviable situation who are gradually thrown out of the system without any access to wealth and the basic needs of subsistence.

Therefore the eventual possibility of the poor becoming poorer and the rich becoming richer exists; but to avoid the negative extreme, there is always a "safety-net" to cater for the extreme disadvantaged; through the social benefits system, as it is practiced now in the UK.

Other typical examples to site are in countries like India and a few Latin American countries such as Brazil, Peru and Nicaragua. As they have a large number of poor, they have a public distribution system in place with governments' subsidised fixed prices to protect the poor.

Free market economy is often associated with a Capitalistic Economy where means of productions are privately owned. This practically gives rise to encouragement of entrepreneurships, forging like minded individuals to work hard to produce more and create employment for others. They assist their governments in jobs creation and help to fight unemployment.

Call for a shift in the UK provision of education services:

Until recently, Kealey (2006) discovers that application of socialism to the provision of educational services and allocation of resources has not been in the best interest of the state.

In comparing with the American counterpart institutions, Dr Terence Kealey (2993) highlights the reasons as to why American universities are superior to ours, and other economically advantaged nations. He states that the aim of all universities must be to move away from state dependence to independence.

> *"The best universities in the world are independent, but in the UK we've made the mistake of allowing governments to fund—and therefore control—the universities directly. The Higher Education Funding Councils should be abolished, and the universities should be freed of state control. The HEFCs' funds should be transferred to needs blind funding agencies to allow students, regardless of background, to access higher education on the grounds solely of merit."*
> *Kealey elaborated.*

Supported by Marek Hlavac (2008), who argues for a radical overhaul of the UK school system calls for a universal open access scheme and to allow parents to send their children to school of their choice; being faith, private or state owned and at the same time assisting eligible ones with state funding on a per-pupil basis as practiced in Sweden.

All of these ideas are in support of the free market economy, which primarily is a system where the buyer and sellers are solely responsible for the choices they make.

Absolute power to prices is given to the free market economy determined by the forces of demand and supply of a respective commodity.

In cases of demand falling short of the supply of a respective commodity, the price will fall as opposed to a price rise when the supply is inadequate to meet the growing demand of a good or service.

On the other hand, totalitarian (communist) economies or Socialistic Economies like the erstwhile USSR, China and North Korea, till date with government regulated system, have prices of goods and services totally administered by their governments'.

Socialistic countries, such as parts of the erstwhile Soviet Republic like Ukraine, Belarus and Lithuania are gradually coming out of the Communist shadow and moving towards a free market economy.

Capitalistic Economies have the biggest advantage of giving people what they deserve rather than either "putting everybody in the same plane or putting all eggs in one basket'. Success of countries practicing free market is only evident with the growth of the USA, the Scandinavian countries, Germany and France as major world powers. Countries such as India and China, by allowing liberalization of its trade to some extent and practicing free market principles brought about more efficiency among its domestic producers and increased its growth rate markedly.

Free market existing with the doctrines of Socialism like limited regulation of prices by the government to protect the poor can be an ideal situation for developing countries *like India, China and South East Asian counties, as well as Sierra Leone, The Gambia and other African countries to attain growth and prosperity.*

In the provision of services by the British government, there have been a series of instances where most industries have been privatised simply to create competition among service providers. One of the cases to site, of privatisation according to Atkinson and Miller (1998), is the services of the bus industry.

Local Authorities provided bus services in UK for many years until when the Conservative government discovered that the system was not profitable and thereafter, privatised the services which led to breaking up the national bus company, introducing fierce competition among the bus service companies and further encouraged new entrants.

This eventually allowed market forces to determine the structure of the industry, a theory also established academically by the Harvard professor, Michael Porter in his competitive advantage, Porter, (1994).

As competition spreads over all industries as symbol of challenge for success, educational institutions are also included. In the last two decades, education has been re-structured by the introduction of market competition. This has created a situation that has resulted into a series of impact on resource management in educational institutions giving birth to additional responsibilities on managers dealing with these institutions. As Rachel Patterson writes (March 2009)

> *'Today, many industrialised nations have developed a multitude of social programmes, and these have become so entrenched that theorists, and politicians alike, claim the 'right' of citizens to their services. We are told we have a right to health care, education, unemployment insurance, and so on. Indeed, Jack Straw, the UK Justice Minister, recently proposed to codify these entitlements in a new British Bill of Rights. But do we, as citizens of developed nations, actually have these rights?'*

Elaborating on the concepts of right, Rachel further elucidated on its development since the 17th and 18th century and sited the natural rights of humans to their own life and a freedom to socially contract with one another for protection and unto other forms of rights such as liberty and property in addition to natural rights.

In the free market economy business organisations are always engaged in planning and developing strategies to increasing their sales volume and to reflect on possibilities of profit maximisation. This has further given rise to understanding buying behaviour of people for the professional practice of marketing which starts with understanding of customers' wants and their level of demand power; their ability and willingness to pay for the products or services when completed and introduced in the market.

Educational institutions in UK such as the Copeland College of Science and Technology in Wembley, North West London caters for many areas of interests on their curricula and one of such significant areas attracting high level of interests is the training in Information Technology.

As Market Report 2009 published by Key Note Report 2009 (B6583124), explains the requirements for training in Information Technology (IT), if training vendors in IT are to succeed, attention should be paid on training given to boost and improve IT skills focusing on the following areas:

- the use, maintenance and repair of data-processing equipment and peripherals
- computer programming and the maintenance of programmes
- the use of packaged software applications
- the implementation and running of systems (e.g. computer networks)
- other related areas (e.g. providing It professionals with business skills to allow them to operate as consultants).

Copland College as a market sector for such product, in order to attract customers should focus on the:

1. Instructor-Led Training "ILT" meaning that the instructor is always present during the training provision to provide more

confidence and satisfaction to the buyers (students or sponsors). The report further says that:

'ILT comprises formal courses that are run at the training provider's premises and tailored courses that are usually performed at the customer's premises. Former courses are important as they determine the structure on which all other types of courses are based; they are considered to account for the bulk of the IT training market.

Tailored courses are predominantly used by large corporations and organisations. Staffs are usually trained on the client's own premises and the courses typically focus on non IT professionals (e.g. end users of IT systems) and cover areas such as training on software packages'.

2. E-Learning where instructor is not present in person: This includes multimedia compact disk-interactive (CD-i), computer based training CBT) and Internet-based online training courses also, covering distance learning courses with a substantial element of electronic content. However, ILT is the more important of the two teaching methods, because it offers and provides face-to-face interaction between the trainer and the trainee, as well as providing opportunity for the trainee to ask questions as the course progresses.

MARKET TRENDS OF "IT" TRAINING:

The market for IT training is usually affected by economic downturns and 2009 is, therefore, expected to be a difficult year according to the 2009 Key Note report on Training for IT.

According to the November 2008 annual issue of the Financial Services Report London, (IFSL Research B6583124) on Financial

Services Education and Training, the UK has a long tradition of supplying education and training services to international students and professionals through professional institutions, pre-employment education services offered by universities, business schools and further education colleges as well as private specialist training firms and industry associations.

As the UK is not the only supplier in the education market internationally, it means that there is a competitive platform on which the UK is "dancing" with other suppliers like the USA, Canada, Russia, Australia, France, Japan etc. However, the report further reveals that the UK's success has been over the years triggered by a variety of factors and distribution channels.

The facilitating role of the British Council and the establishments of websites such as (www.educationuk.org and www.cityoflondonlearning. org) are high commended for high profile public relations organ for UK government.

The strengths of UK providers in the international education supply markets are mainly the development of strong global reputation of UK education and training services especially focusing on:

i. Historical reputation: As many of the UK professional education institutions and universities have an established track record, perhaps even over a century, for providing vocational and occupational qualifications that are internationally recognised.

ii. International orientation: Many institutions and universities in UK have in the beginning focused on establishing international orientation by designing and delivering courses to adapt and apply in other countries around the world relating to:

a. *International membership.* Many professional bodies and academic educational institutions of UK origins have a significant proportion of membership based in other countries providing consultation and other engagement activities relating to membership and practice.

b. *International Partnership.* Many UK institutions have established partnership agreements with other or similar institutions locally in other countries and this gives them the opportunity to establish their presence to sell their values, profession and discipline. Fourah Bay College, for example (now one of the constituent colleges of the University of Sierra Leone through a Royal Charter of 1960) was once affiliated to the UK's University of Durham since 1876. (www.fourahbaycollege.net/index).

c. *International Students.* The OECD (Education at a Glance) reported in 2008 that "the UK accounted for 11% of 2.9 million international students being educated at the tertiary level in a country other than their home country.

The UK was second only to the US, with Germany, France and Australia being the next most popular destination countries. Also, there is a broad multinational spread of students coming to the UK and between 2000 and 2001, 2006 and 2007 the number of international students studying in the UK rose by 52% to reach more than 351,000, with the largest increase from new developing markets in Asia (particularly China and India) and Africa as well as more recently from Eastern Europe."

Countries of origin of international students in UK Tertiary education

Countries	2000/01	2006/07	% change
China	12095	49595	310
Greece	31150	49595	-48

India	4875	23835	389
Ireland	13510	16255	20
US	9425	15955	69
Germany	11370	14010	23
France	9950	13070	31
Malaysia	10005	11810	18
Nigeria	2650	11135	320
Hong Kong	8335	9640	16
Cyprus	4030	8710	116
Pakistan	2210	9305	321
Taiwan	4525	6795	50
Poland	600	6770	1028
Spain	5860	6350	8
Italy	5415	5990	11
Japan	6154	5705	-7
Other	88711	120490	
Total	**230870**	**351470**	

Source: UK Higher Education Statistics Agency

iii. <u>Integrated Structure and relevance of qualifications:</u> The integrated structure of educational institutions programmes provides entry and progression movement routes to achieve variety of qualifications to levels of preferences such as chartered/professional as well as bachelors, postgraduates and doctorate qualification status.

iv. <u>Presence of modular structure</u>:

The presence of modular structure in UK education system, engineered by practitioners drawn from across different industries and disciplines who devise and monitor examinations, allows for choice in pursuit of qualifications.

The institutions are actively involved in continuous review of their education curricula to fit in, with changes and to ensure provision for adaptation of training and qualifications, making it possible to meet requisite standards both in the UK and overseas.

v.   <u>Opportunity for professional development:</u> Another advantage in UK education system is the presence of professional development. UK universities and professional education providers offer broad range of training and continuous learning opportunities in order to ensure that professionals are able to update and update their core competencies.

This system has even given birth to what is now popularly known as Life-Long Learning or Post Compulsory Education taking place in the FE Sector colleges.

vi. Strict monitoring and accountability of government powers:

Resources allocated to those state approved educational institutions are continuously inspected and monitored by the Office for Standard in Education (Ofsted) for accountability of the funding they receive. As money for this funding comes from British taxpayers, it is therefore prerogative of government to ensure that it is properly accounted for by ensuring that it is properly spent on relevant educational courses and not misappropriated. Recently, the principal, Sir Alan Davies resigned and the vice Dr. Richard Evans sacked, at the Copeland College in Wembley for unaccounted funds (more than £1.00m) as reported by *Harrow Times (Tuesday 5th November 2009)*.

Management as Nickels, et al (1987) defines, is a process that is used to accomplish organizational goals; that is a process that is used to achieve what an organization, either a business, a school, social club, government hospital, etc wants to achieve. Managers are the people to this management is assigned, and it is generally thought that they achieve the desired goals through the key functions of, planning, organizing, directing, controlling and budgeting (which could also be part of planning).

Many different activities take place in all organisations. In a retail store (such as Tesco), for example, there are people who buy merchandise to sell, people to sell merchandise, people who prepare the merchandise for display, people who are responsible for the advertising and promotion, people to do the accounting work, people who hire and train employees, and many other workers. There might be one manager for the entire store, but there are other managers at different levels who are more directly responsible for the people who perform all other jobs.

At each level of management, the key functions are included. The emphasis change with each different level of manager.

Managers of educational institutions are all engaged in the practice of management functions. The Office for Standards in Education, Children's Services and Skills (Ofsted) is the UK organisation responsible for regulating and inspecting registered childcare and children's social care, including adoption and fostering agencies, residential schools, family centres and homes for children.

It also inspects all state maintained schools, non-association independent schools, pupil referred units, further education, initial teacher education, and *publicly funded* adult skills and employment based training, the Children and Family Court Advisory and Support Services (Cafcass), and the overall level of services for children in local authority areas (through annual performance assessment and joint area reviews).

In addition with Raising Standards, Improving Lives, an Ofted publication of October 2008-Reference No. 080200, Ofsted began a broad programme of inspection development with the underpinning rationale to ensure that:

1. inspection focus sharply on improvement, particularly the outcomes for and the needs of underachieving groups and those in vulnerable circumstances.
2. they encourage the services they inspect to focus on the interests of children and parents who use the services.
3. the services they inspect are efficient and effective.

This simply means that all educational institutions receiving government or public funding (maintained schools) are under Ofsted inspection which also varies from time to time according to an Ofsted evaluation document *"A focus on improvement proposals for maintained school inspections from September 2009"*. (www.ofsted. gov.uk/publications/070179).

Ofsted further stated that they intend to continue to reduce the scale of inspection for the best schools to enable them to focus their efforts where they have the greatest impact.

As there are many institutions under Ofsted inspection, competition to meet Ofsted expectation for successful report recommendation is fiercely increasing in order to meet funding recommendations which has caused high level of market competition among those educational institutions.

Competition, by definition, is a combat between individuals, groups, nations, animals, etc. for territory, a niche or allocation of resources or supplies. Competition usually arises whenever two or more parties strive for a goal which cannot be shared.

Market competition among government maintained educational institutions in UK for Ofsted supports usually occurs as they are co-existing in the same environment. They are in competition with one another over the same group of students who are otherwise the customers of these institutions.

As the volume of Ofsted supports is highly attracted by the number (volume) of students, institutions are now-a-days targeting top appearance on league tables to attract more students.

Interestingly enough, less developed areas described as being deprived, have in the past received more funding to support community education development, led to construction of State Academy schools in UK.

As marketing is a management process responsible for anticipating, stimulating and satisfying customer requirements profitably according to the UK Chartered Institute of Marketing, Kotler (1994) explains that the essence of production of goods and services is to satisfy customer requirements profitably. Therefore, educational institutions introduce new course programmes because there are interested students and also that the environments in which courses are offered is ergonomic enough to facilitate the learning process. Additionally, is the availability of trained and qualified teaching and administrative professional staffs, mandatory in all schools in UK (early learning, primary and secondary), through "Qualified Teaching Status-QTS" minimum qualification requirement.

BIBLIOGRAPHY

1. Adam Smith (1776) The Wealth of Nations World Book Encyclopedia, USA

2. Atkinson & Miller (1998) Business Economics Prentice Hall(Times Magazine)

3. Finacial Services Report: IFL Research B6583124 (November 2009)

4. Galick and Urwick (1973) The New Education (1910-1914) Sir Isaac Pitman &Sons, Melbourne.

5. Harek and Hlavac (2008) Open Access to UK Schools House Magazine (January 16 2008)

6. Harrow Times (Tuesday 5 November 2009)

7. Key Note Report: B6583124 (2009)

8. Kotler, P. (1994), Marketing: (Analysis, Planning, Implementation and Control) Eith Edition. Paramount Communications Company, Englewood Cliffs, New Jersey, 07652, USA

9. Market Report (2009)

10. Michael Porter(1985) Competitive Advantage Free Press, USA

11. Nickels, et al (1987)

12. Rachel Paterson (March 2009) A Short History of the Social Right Myths. Adam Smith Institute.

13. T. Kealey (2003) Transforming Higher Education. Adam Smith Institute

14. UK Higher Education Statistics Agency

15. www.educationuk.org

16. www.cityoflondonlearning.org

17. www.fourahbaycollege.net/index

18. www.ofsted.gov.uk/publications

MODULE FIVE

Human Resource Issues In Education

Assignment Title:

"How do the three 'perspectives' on the nature of the employment relationship help us to understand why the management of human resources in education be sometimes appear to be 'the management of the unmanageable'?"

In your discussion, please refer to a case study of an HR initiative or ongoing issue in your own organization (for example pay/job evaluation/ appraisal, or skillmix/reprofiling/professional autonomy, or equalities, or workload/worklife balance/absenteeism, or job security/redundancy/ outsourcing, or part-time/flexible working, etc.) You should also make full reference to the literature in the module where relevant.

> *Please note your case study 'issue' should be agreed in principle with the tutor before you leave today if it is not included in these examples.*

(3,000-3,500 words)

Introduction

Human Resources Issues (HRI) are very important and have now become major issues in employment and industrial relation in every industry. This simply means that both industrialist and employees usually agree on terms and conditions in which they should work when coming together and that these terms and conditions are usually set and made known to the understanding of both parties before the commencement of employment. Where any part of the agreement is not agreeable or favourable to any party, there is always cause to raise and ask for negotiation.

Human Resource Issues are now calling attention for detail discussions that are far beyond the Human Resources Management (HRM), as they now require more knowledge beyond management skills to leadership capability. Writers of management define their subject as the art of getting a task completed with the aid of utilising people, resources and finance, according to Beardwell and Holden (1997) but leadership is stated as "process of social influence in which one person can enlist the aid and support of others in the accomplishment of a common task". Allan Keith of Geretech stated that "leadership is ultimately about creating a way for people to contribute to making something extraordinary happen." (www.wikipedia.org). "A leader is the one who knows the way, goes the way and shows the way", as John C. Maxwell simply puts it.

Which of the leaders we have ever got in Sierra Leone since independent that we can boast have come closer these leadership dispensations with the exception of Sir Milton Margai?

Ernest Bai Koroma's leadership according to his first presidential speech is focused on business management because he was once a manager of an insurance company. This is the leader who invests the nation's money on electricity with no financial returns because the country needs electricity supply even when such service cannot be sustained as long as his party's supports and profile remain high. One could therefore imagine that thorough understanding of strategic policy is a very strong vital tool every manager must master in management principles in order to succeed and remain on track.

Leadership, though not easy to explain and practice, is about behaviour first, and skills second. Good leaders are followed chiefly because people trust and respect them, rather than the skills they possess. Leadership is further different from management. Management relies on management skills too, but more so on qualities such as integrity, honesty, humility, courage, commitment, sincerity, passion, confidence, wisdom, determination, compulsion, sensitivity and degree of personal charisma.

The success of leadership starts with the way leaders think. This paper is being present to discuss these issues that are involved and raised in this very important topic, the Human Relations Issues (HRI) with particular reference to educational institutions, although some slight scratches are made on politics, particularly the West African politics, but focusing on educational discussions.

Mohamed Sannoh, University of Keele, U.K

There are different types of style of management ideologies that are usually focused when discussing management issues relating to industrial relations and these construct the beginning of "rationalist ethical theories" according to Kimberley Hutchings (2010) which are discussed as flows:

Utilitarian Ethics: Known as the consequentialist ethical theory, it argues that the moral worth of particular ethical values and principles depends on the goodness or badness of the outcomes of adopting those principles for individual human beings and aggregates of individual human beings. This simply bases on the assumptions of what motivates and satisfies human beings naturally and that when these attributes are discovered, it is important to cater for them in the work place for human satisfaction, although these may counteract the religious ethics already in people. Therefore, Utilitarianism is most well known and influential form of consequentialist ethics as agreed by Petit(1993) and Shaw (2006).

The United Kingdom, for example (and from personal observation) is officially declared and known to be a Christian religious state and the Monarch, in the person of the Queen, is officially the "the defender of the faith, the Christian faith". However, social lobbyist have been able to put forward the gay and lesbian rights to be accepted and recognized in society which has now given rise to single sex marriages (a woman getting married to a woman or a man getting married to a man; of the same sex) in Britain, which the churches are finding difficult to accept, although the Anglican church still remain in the grey area with this practice. The Labour government accepted this in order to cater for people in that bracket, bring them the satisfaction they need and thus winning their votes. Also, because of the multiculturalism of Britain, so many different religions have arrived in the country of recent years and this has given rise to many mosques and Hindu temples as landmarks in many parts of the boroughs, such as Brent with the largest Hindu Temple in Europe at Neasden and couple of Hindu Temples in South Hall in London, the capital of this Christian country. Therefore, the Monarch is no longer practically the "defender of the faith, the Christian faith" but the defender of faiths, as a result of the multicultural acceptance of Britain. So you see, this ethical theory of defending the faith, has drawn a qualitative distinction between what motivates ethics or morality on one hand and the gratification of individual, selfish desires on the other hand, as Hutchings(2010) put it.

The founder of Utilitarian Ethics, Bentham (1748-1832) argues that human beings are naturally driven towards pleasure and happiness and away from pain and unhappiness. Therefore, all human beings are by nature, pleasure seeking animals. As far as Bentham is concerned, moral behaviour is simply the act of impartiality to promote and to achieve the desires of many peoples happiness as possible. This principle has now become political mantra of many political parties in Britain including the Labour party that led the Prime Minister, Tony Blair to take on board the legalization of single sex marriage (civil partnership) with all rights, privileges and benefits in Britain.

Utilitarianism has for centuries faced heavy criticisms from other utilitarian thinkers such as J.S. Mill(1806-1873) by pointing out that utilitarianism is becoming unethical because it could justify the misery of a small number of people to promote the happiness of many, giving rise to social corruption in some countries where some minority tribes are deprived from development such as education to give space to those in the majority.

In the West African state of The Gambia, for example, the former government under President Dauda Jawara did not make any provision for university education in the country. Those Gambians who received university education were selected from the Madinka tribe, (the majority tribe in The Gambia) and sent to the University of Sierra Leone for higher education and only those chosen ones were identified for leadership roles in the country. As far as Jawara's state of mind was concerned, only those from the Madinka tribe were designed to occupy leadership roles in the country and all other tribes were servants. Those who received university educations outside the Madinka tribal origin were able do so through philanthropist chances and mainly from extended family members outside the country, possibly at overseas to sponsor their education.

When Yahya Jammeh, a young body guard military major from a very minority Jola tribe succeeded in a palace coup, one of his civilised first ventures was to open higher education facilities for ALL Gambia nationals, through the establishment of the University of The Gambia, first of its kind in the country. Secondly, there was only one national radio station during the Jawara regime that was controlled by the government. Therefore, the broadcast of that station was edited by government agency; but President Yahya Jammeh has now opened the Gambia Radio and Television Service (GRTS) and many other radio stations in addition to the former Gambia Radio. As Jawara had a utilitarian thinking, Jammeh's thinking has proved totally different, perhaps more nationalistic. The seal of this thinking is the spill over effect on the country.

My personal perception of The Gambia is the emergence of total development as they prepare every national, a total tribal inclusion in the challenges of every aspect of leadership through the University of The Gambia (The UniGam). Therefore, Yahya Jammeh has got it right. I like him personally for that. He is a door opener for African patriotism and a model for true leadership.

Whether Yahya Jammeh has been successful in The Gambia or not, could hardly depends on the style of leadership he is applying. He did not do the same mistake Valentine Strasser did in Sierra Leone, by inviting corrupt politicians he overthrew to work with. My personal admiration about that guy is that he has introduced a new dimension of democratic politics in his own right in Africa. All of us in Africa are crying for good governance and a leader that is poised for development, especially in education, infrastructure and good standard of life. Whether any Gambian wants to appreciate this or not, those of us who are visitors in The Gambia begin to appreciate and show gratitude to Yahya Jammeh's leadership as a real modern African president. It is therefore saddened to read some of Gambian opinions in the foreign press about their president, just for the fact that he has overstayed since he ousted Sir Dauda Jawara in 1994. Within this period however, there is no more potholes in the streets of Banjul and at least, there is now traffic lights at Kairaba Avenue and street lights from the airport. If The Gambians are tired of Jammeh, can we please have him in Sierra Leone for just one month? Whenever there is a nomination for Africa

Leadership for the continent, I will be the first to nominate Yahya Jammeh.

At this point, let me elaborate more on leadesrship styles as shared by Marcels De Resende at the Kaplan Open Learning of Essex University in UK.

There will be many times in ones educational career when you will be called upon to lead a discussion group or a project.

There are several different approaches to being an effective boss or project leader. Some people are born with a natural style and some can learn to mould their behaviour to fit any situation. Understanding each style is important in order to maximize your leadership skills. Do you know which style you have? Do you know how and when to alter your leadership style?

There are four major types of student leadership roles. You will find that there is an appropriate time and place for each style. As you progress in your studies, you may want to learn skills and techniques from each leadership style.

Autocratic Leadership

This form of leadership is one of the least desirable when it comes to building trusting relationships and making friends! In a system of autocratic leadership, one person has control over all of the workers or followers. The leader is in complete control and no one is permitted to make any suggestions or offer any opinions, no matter how it may benefit the group.

When it comes to leading a group in school or in a group project, you will find that autocratic leadership can make you very unpopular. If communication and trust are important, you don't want to lean too far toward autocratic leadership.

But there is a time when autocratic traits can prove beneficial. This form of leadership is effective when absolute control is needed over a group. Have you ever worked on a group project that fell flat? That happens when no strong leader is present.

__Benefits of Autocratic Leadership__

Group projects require strong leadership. Without it, nobody gets a full understanding of what is required of anybody else. Unfortunately, that often means that some group members procrastinate and wait for others to do the work. In the end, the project suffers (and so does your grade!).

If your group plans to work online at all, you should really think about electing a strong leader. This leader should be willing to take charge, divide the work, and set deadlines. He or she must take full control. Communication is difficult enough when it comes to group work, but when technology is involved it often breaks down completely.

If your group attempts to communicate via email or other electronic communication, strong leadership is an absolute must! It is wise, when working in a group, to assign a strong leader with some autocratic tendencies.

A typical autocratic leader was Siaka Probyn Stevens, who was the first Prime Minister of Sierra Leone from 1967 to 1971 and the 1st President from 1971 to 1985. Many of his political opponents were executed, but on a positive note, he reduced the ethnic polarization in the government of Sierra Leone by incorporating members of various ethnic groups in his dominating All Peoples Congress (APC) before his death on 29 May 1988.

Bureaucratic Leadership

This style of leadership follows a close set of standards. Everything is done in an exact, specific way to ensure safety and/or accuracy. You will often find this leadership role in a situation where the work environment is dangerous and specific sets of procedures are necessary to ensure safety.

In the working world bureaucratic leadership skills would be best utilized in jobs such as construction work, chemistry-related jobs that involve working with hazardous material, or jobs that involve working with large amounts of money.

Benefits of Bureaucratic Leadership

In school work, you may find that bureaucratic leadership skills are necessary when working on a group project for a science class. Precision is key in a science project, and meticulous notes are essential.

A natural bureaucratic leader will tend to create detailed instructions for other members of a group. This type of leader would also be very successful working in student government roles.

Charismatic Leadership

A Charismatic leader is one who provides an environment full of energy and positive reinforcement. If you are naturally charismatic, you are very fortunate! This is a trait that is not so easily learned.

Charismatic leaders inspire others and encourage them to be their best. Employees and group members want to impress a charismatic leader, so they work hard and strive to succeed.

Although Foday Sankoh, Leader of the rebel group, the Revolutionary United Front (RUF) was not very popular in the politics of Sierra Leone, he will always be remembered as a charismatic leader among his followers. He had the charisma to get his followers do what he expected of them to do and produce results. That is all what charismatic leadership is about and Foday Sankoh possessed those qualities.

The RUF nearly ceased to exist when he was imprisoned in Nigeria. In fact many people in Sierra Leone thought that the name Foday Sankoh was a myth and he does not even exist, until when he was finally repatriated back into Sierra Leone by Sani Abacha, the then Nigerian leader.

The mistake of the Sierra Leone government, on Foday Sankoh's arrival was parading him on the national television with his hands in cuffs. This was proved to be high profile publicity and a national meeting point to communicate with his followers that he was back and still alive.

He received this free of charge and he immediately took advantage of the situation to register that he was a force to recon with and a voice to listen to on national decision making for Sierra Leone. However, since Foday Sankoh died in prison in 2002, it appears that he entered his grave with RUF because there has been no noise from that camp in Sierra Leone.

Whether anybody likes it or not, Adolf Hitler was another charismatic leader of the Nazi movement in Germany during the World War II.

He was able to command his followers to the fullest and continued lying to them, repeatedly that the cause of hardships in Germany was due to the presence of the Jews and the only solution was to extinct their existence and his followers believed him very well.

They believed him not because he was saying the truth, but because he repeatedly told lies about the Jews and because his followers respected him and looked up to him; he ruled them to total destruction.

In his last few days and in his last few hours, Hitler noticed that he was totally surrounded by the allies and because he noticed that there was no way to escape, he took refuge in a bunker with his children, closed inner circle members and where he also married one of his concubines. At the end he ordered the killing of his children and committed suicide together with his wife in fear of what would happen to him and his family if they were to fall into enemy hands.

Pitfalls of Charismatic Leadership

Under charismatic leadership, group members may view success in relation to their leaders. A major problem with charismatic leadership is that group success tends to hinge on the leader. The charismatic leader is the glue that holds a group together. So what happens if the leader should have to step down or transfer? Normally, the group dynamic will fizzle and individual members will lose enthusiasm.

When Is Charismatic Leadership Most Useful?

Charismatic leadership is great for short-term projects. As long as you are working on a task that can be completed in a semester, you don't have to worry so much about your group falling apart with the loss of leadership.

Charismatic leaders are great for projects that require energy and talent. Drama assignments, writing assignments, sports-related tasks, art projects—these activities could be very successful when led by a charismatic person.

Can charisma be learned? Charisma is a special quality that people possess that serves as a magnet, of sorts, but it is really made up of many traits. One of the most important elements is self-confidence. People who appear confident instill confidence in those around them. Another element of charisma is great communication ability—and that starts with a strong and effective vocabulary.

It would be a great idea to build upon those elements to make you as charismatic as possible!

DEMOCRATIC LEADERSHIP:

Under democratic leadership, the people have a more participatory role in the decision making process. One person retains final say over all decisions but allows others to share insight and ideas.

This is often a highly effective form of leadership. People are more likely to excel in their positions and develop more skills when they feel empowered, and people are empowered when they are involved in the decision-making process.

Although it may take some time to achieve full participation from a group, the end result will be rewarding if you can manage to establish a power-sharing environment in your group project. You will find that democratic practices often lead to a more productive and higher quality work group.

Examples of democratic leadership:

- Asking all group members for ideas and input.
- Voting on the best course of action in a project.
- Asking group members to work with their strengths and provide input on how to divide the work.]li]Enabling members to work at their own pace and set their own deadlines.

Pitfalls of Democratic Leadership

It doesn't take too much imagination to think of ways that democratic leadership could backfire during a group project. As you probably know, some members of a group will work well, on their own and complete all work in a timely fashion. But there are other workers who will procrastinate—and that can lead to disaster. The former president of Sierra Leone, Mr. Ahmed Tejan Kabbah, could be sited as a typical example here. However, although he was successful in his leadership style, his administration suffered from a lot of detractors' mainly from the political party he represented, The Sierra Leone Peoples Party (SLPP) and the Civil Defense Force (The "Kamajors") whose activities came to his interest during the civil war.

Further to what contributed to Mr. Kabbah's success, his time of coming to power was during the civil war and very strategic for Sierra Leone. (He is therefore the war time president, the "Winston Churchill of Sierra

Leone" that continued giving hope to all Sierra Leoneans till the end, a successful end). He was nationally strategic because of his extensive contacts, especially with Kofi Annan personally, the then Secretary General of the United Nation, where Kabbah served for many years, personal supports of George Bush, the then US president and Tony Blair who was also head of Britain at that time. In fact Tony Blair became so interested in Sierra Leone affairs that he sent the late Robin Cook, the then British Foreign Secretary and Clair Short, another British heavy weight in charge of overseas development to survey situations in Sierra Leone before paying two strategic visits to Sierra Leone, himself. Tony Blair's interest in Sierra Leone dated as far back as when his father once served the country in a teaching contract at Fourah Bay College when affiliated to Durham University in UK.

Another reason for President Kabbah being strategic, as I view, was that he was the right leader for Sierra Leone with the right strategic tactics to fight the Sierra Leone civil war to the end and that was why he quitted the political stage and brought Ernest Bai Koroma's APC regime to power in 2007, nearly immediately the war ended. I respect him personally because he did not force to stay in power till death, as Siaka Stevens almost did. *My personal analysis of President Tejan Kabbah is that he never became a politician even when he was the President of Sierra Leone, but a western diplomat and indeed, a civilised gentleman, with a life-style, not for Sierra Leone standard. He stepped on many toes even within the Sierra Leone peoples Party (SLPP), the political party he represented, in the process of doing the right thing to gain everlasting peace which all Sierra Leoneans now enjoy. He was yet, the only African leader who decided to help the rebels out of trouble even when they ran after his life. His reason was because even the rebel leader, Foday Sankoh "did not know what he was doing" Were those not the same words Jesus told his prosecutors during the last few minutes of his life on the cross at Calvary as recorded in Luke, Chapter 23:34?*

Who is this man called Ahmed Tejan Kabbah? Is he a Christian but dressed in a Muslim robe? I was in London when he got the first coup from Johnny Paul Koroma. Immediately that day, Dr. Abass Bundu was highly engaged on the telephone and sending faxes to the "new rulers" to state house, urging them not to give up or step down and that he was backing them up all the way. He advised them that the Nigerian soldiers (ecomog) had no right to intervene into the internal affairs of Sierra Leone and that was against the ECOWAS agreement. One Sunday afternoon, he called a meeting of Sierra Leoneans at a church hall in North London during which he addressed the delegates on the same issue. Upon the restoration of President Kabbah into state house later by the Ecomog soldiers, some of Dr. Abass Bundu's faxes he sent to the Junta's government were found intact by Tejan Kabbah. The renegade Dr. Abass Bundu was also wanted in Sierra Leone to account for a number of national passports he sold for twenty dollars each, to mostly Chinese seamen who immediately became Sierra Leoneans upon the possession of those identities.

I was also in The Gambia when President Kabbah paid a state visit there in 2002 when Alusine Fofannah was the Sierra Leone High Commissioner. One of the delegates that received President Kabbah was Dr. Abass Bundu to whom President Kabbah spoke and reassured that he would be protected if he was to return home. As I write, Dr. Abass Bundu is in Sierra Leone and still participating in party politics on the side of SLPP and perhaps he would even become the party leader and contest in a Presidential election.

Let's talk about Tejan Kabbah again. There is another side of the coin which I heard by hearsay, although specific proofs are yet to reveal. Is it true that Tejan Kabbah was in fact the legal adviser to All Peoples Congress (APC) party in Sierra Leone for years before the Bintumani Conference in Freetown that brought him victory for the Sierra Leone Peoples Party (SLPP) leadership in 1996? How did he do it? What happened between Tejan Kabbah and Hinga Norman? Was it the same skills of ability to play the raw African political game? Why was Tejan Kabbah so silence, especially in the months and weeks that followed the 2007 General Election when in fact he continued hanging on the presidential baton and pushed Solomon Berewa into the race alone, without coming out to canvass for his SLPP party he has graciously enjoyed? If he had wanted to help Solomon Berewa, his Vice President why did he not transfer power to him at least one year before the 2007 general election day? Was he afraid of being held tight to the corner of being called to answer some pressing questions within the party handling? Can this Tejan Kabbah man be trusted with Ernest Koroma?

Some analyst still believes that the APC victory of 2007 that took Ernest Bai Koroma to state house was a hanky-panky sellout of SLPP by Tejan Kabbah to APC. He is therefore accountable to SLPP whenever the party comes to power, especially under Maada Bio's presidency. As the saying goes, hit the iron when it is hot if only you want to shape it properly. If the British government is taking members of parliament to court and have, them jailed for crimes committed, I see no reason why Sierra Leonean politicians cannot stand for justice in the defense of common good.

If you are a natural democratic leader, it might be necessary to learn some traits of the autocratic or bureaucratic leaders and tap into them as necessary. Always have a backup plan on hand! Although however, he has beautifully decorated his sitting room, Yahya Jammeh still encourages some traces of skeletons in his cupboard that needs checking, well before they begin to smell to the inconvenience of his visiting guests. As for example, the establishment of the National Training Authority (NTA) in 2002 could be considered as the introduction of radical practices to coincide with radical changes in putting checks on vocational institutions, one could judge heavily that he was not well advised on some of the radical changes the NTA is implementing on privately run institutions where government makes no contribution.

Tertiary education is although developing, but still at its infancy in The Gambia, closing down privately run foreign institutions for not installing air conditions into classrooms is just very ridiculous when even the government classrooms are as hot as the room next to hell but one can understand when such institutions are largely run by foreign nationals interested in educational development in the country.

The Gambia still depends largely on foreign aids and investment in all aspects of development including education. As Yahya Jammeh has openly put this forward in the Vision 2020 Document, committing all Gambia nationals, fixing the grudge on owners of institutions run by non-Gambians thinking that they are profiting more is not benefiting anyone in the country including Yahya Jammeh himself.

Investment in education is investment on human resources and thus on the development of the nation. Instead of closing down foreign institutions, the Gambian government should explore solutions of assisting their development.

Finally, it is in the good interest of Gambians to remain friendly, not as enemies of its neighbours in the sub-region. What happened in the case of Kenneth Best's investment in the Daily Observer, the Gambian Groundnut Corporation (GGC) investment in farming, the Ahmaddiyya Muslim Missions investments in education and hospitals, Tony Cantoni's investment into the restaurant business and much, much more are still raw in the minds of many interested investors, although a forgotten history in the Gambian minds. All these memoirs involve foreign investors.

On the twentieth-century debates over the merits of utilitarianism as a moral philosophy, it is common philosophy of the politics of some West African states to apply thugs and implement the deaths and torture few innocents, they say, may be justified in the light of the achievement of the happiness of many.

Some readers have even subjected totalitarianism to be compatible with lying, stealing and cheating as long as these actions are promoted for the happiness of greater number of people. "Where they tie cow is where it should graze" was the instigating statement of one West African head of state that corrupted many civil servants to steel as much as they could in their ministries where they worked.

Political and social corruption grew so much in that country that things went out of hands to the point of breaking into civil war that lasted for ten years causing many lives and people still displaced.

The United Nations statistics shows that the country, despites the availability of minerals including gold, diamond, etc. is today classed among the poorest and the least mortality rate with the average age of 35 years (although this may not be accurate).

Corruption has so much rooted in that country that even the politicians and top civil servants finds it difficult to cope without illegitimate practices and that was why they voted against the political party that wanted to put things right such as the introduction of free examination fees for all secondary school children, enabling children from large families to complete schooling with examination qualifications to move on in life.

The current corrupt government cuts discontinued that education assistance to families for the fact that families should take the burden of educating their children. My perception for that country is a lead into darkness for the simple fact that only the selected few are opened to education, through government cuts on educational facilities, not affordable by all. Therefore, education is now left opened only to the "haves" and <u>NOT</u> the "have nuts" which is devastating for any country on the surface of the planet earth. My personal judgment is that we have got it wrong in Sierra Leone and we are still getting it wrong especially, through the greed of our politicians, especially the APC politicians, emanating from Siaka Stephens to Momoh and now, to Ernest Bai Koroma.

Despite the reality of calamity in which our country has ever since plunged into since the midnight hour on 27 April 1961 as marked by the lowering of the Union Jack and the hoisting of the Green, White and Blue at the parliament floor of our country, all political heads with the exception of Sir Milton Margai (who took earlier retirement to rest) on 28 April 1964 have never won the "X-Factor" but focused on different fashions corruptions that have turned our country into a retched poor country. The apex of the Sierra Leone chapter of the African politics is narrated exclusively by the speech of J.B. Jenkins-Johnson, Esq, a Freetown Legal practitioner which cannot be left out is this book is to be completed fully and as such, I hereby present some extracts with his pemission:

SIERRA LEONE AT 50:

HOW FAR? HOW NEAR?

BY J.B. JENKINS-JOHNSON ESQ., LEGAL PRACTITIONER

"Mr. President, SLAJ, Members of SLAJ, Distinguished Ladies and Gentlemen, May I firstly take this opportunity to thank you and all your members for inviting me as one of your Discussants, thereby giving me the opportunity to

---

speak to the People of Sierra Leone on this unique and historic occasion.

May I also extend to the President, The Government and the entire People of Sierra Leone hearty and sincere congratulations on the occasion of the 50th Anniversary [Golden Jubilee] of our achievement of Political Independence from our formal Colonial Masters, The United Kingdom on the 27th April 1961.

We achieved Independence peacefully, quietly, and without having to fight a war, after constitutional talks held at Lancaster House in London, England. I sometimes wonder whether the ease with which we did achieve Independence has affected the way we have conducted ourselves as a Nation since 1961. Of that, more anon!

Mr. Chairman, Ladies and Gentlemen, 50 years is a long time in the life of a human being, and using myself as an example, in 50 years from 1961 to 2011, I have metamorphosed from being a fresh-faced 14 year old Schoolboy at the Prince of Wales School, full of hopes, dreams and plans at the time of Independence in 1961, to a 64 year old Grandfather uncertain about the future and wondering what will happen to this Country in the next decade or two. It is an interesting coincidence that even before I received a telephone call from Mr. Umaru Fofanah inviting me to do what I am doing now, I had decided to do an article to be published in the local press on the occasion of The Golden Jubilee of our Independence.

My decision to do so was ignited by something I heard over the BBC at about 5am on Sunday 3rd April 2011. As I lay on my bed listening to "The World Today" a news programme regularly aired over the BBC I heard General Sir Richard

Dannat, the former Head of The British Army, who said he had just returned to Sierra Leone, describe SIERRA LEONE as "A wretchedly poor Country"!! Not a poor country, or even a very poor country—but "A WRETCHEDLY POOR COUNTRY." I must confess that even though I believe the General meant no offence and was just speaking his mind, I immediately felt a deep sense of hurt, anger, offence, outrage and betrayal all rolled up together, not directed at the General, who had not very long ago contributed to saving our Country from disaster, but at ourselves Sierra Leoneans.

As a fiercely patriotic Sierra Leonean who prefers Sierra Leone to anywhere else in the world, I kept asking myself "Are we really a wretchedly poor Country? And indeed, after 50years of Independence ought we to allow ourselves to be in a situation where we are perceived by others as "a wretchedly poor Country? After 50years of Independence with our own Countrymen and women superintending our affairs, ought we to be at or near the bottom of the Human Development Index? After much soul searching, I recalled to mind the immortal words of SHAKESPEARE'S Cassius in his play Julius Caesar, when he said,

"Men at sometime are masters of their fates; The fault Dear Brutus is not in our Stars, but in ourselves, that we are underlings." And that, Mr. Chairman, Ladies and Gentlemen, leads me to the core message of this my contribution today—Since 1961 we have been Masters of our Fate, but what have we done with our Independence, and what have we achieved since 1961? Undoubtedly, there are those who would disagree with me, and they are entitled to their own opinions, but in my respectful submission, we have done precious little

with our independence, and we have achieved precious little since 1961.

OUR NATURAL RESOURCES:

Having regard to the description of Sierra Leone as a "wretchedly poor Country", I now wish to take a brief look at our natural resources just to see why in my most respectful submission we ought not to be in a situation where anyone would even think of describing us as such. Sierra Leone is a relatively small country with a population of not more than Six million [6,000,000] people, blessed with abundant natural resources such as gold, diamonds, rutile, bauxite, iron ore and other minerals; we are further blessed with abundant marine resources such as fish, shrimps, crabs, lobster, etc; we are further blessed with a very rich soil and agricultural produce including Palm kernels, coffee, cocoa, piassava, ginger, etc. We can grow almost anything in Sierra Leone, including vegetables and fruits like cabbage and tomatoes, plantains, oranges, bananas and pineapples. We also have one of the best natural harbours in the world, golden sunshine all the year round, and refreshing rain for about half of the year.

SO WHAT IS WRONG WITH SIERRA LEONE?

And my honest answer is—"THE PEOPLE"—or maybe I should qualify that a bit further, and restate that to be, "THE RULING CLASS" from 1961 to now, and this includes both of The Political Parties who have ruled Sierra Leone since Independence. It has been a litany of "missed opportunities and misplaced priorities."

It is my very carefully considered and researched opinion that in these past 50 years, we as a Nation [through the ruling class] have not harnessed our God-given natural resources for the full benefit of the People of Sierra Leone. What do I mean?

There was a time when we had The Sierra Leone Produce Marketing Board, which was set up to buy produce from local Farmers and Cooperatives and EXPORT same abroad, with the foreign exchange coming back to us—what happened to it? It is said that it was sabotaged by the setting up of other Private Businesses to compete with it. Suffice it to say that as a Nation we no longer export produce and that activity is now in private hands with precious little benefit accruing to the people of the Country. There was a time when we had The National Diamond Mining Company [otherwise known as DIMINCO]; we had the Sierra Leone Selection Trust [SLST]—both engaged in the mining and exportation of diamonds—what happened to them? Well, don't ask me, but suffice it to say they do not exist any longer, mainly because of the selfishness and greed of those who were supposed to be superintending our affairs as a Nation. When will Sierra Leoneans take full charge of our God-given natural resources, and when will we stop giving away our wealth in return for handouts from those who are always ready to exploit our naivety, ineptitude and inadequacies?

I submit to you Ladies and Gentlemen, that unless and until we as Sierra Leoneans decide to harness our own resources for the benefit of our people we will remain "a wretchedly poor Country", going around the world with a begging bowl, leaving others to plunder our wealth.

*To this End, I would recommend that the report of **The Jenkins-Johnston Commission of Inquiry dated 17th March 2008** with particular reference to The Recommendations thereunder BE MADE PUBLIC, so that members of the Public will know what is available to the Government for the* *improvement of our situation so far as the mining industry is concerned, but on which **NO ACTION** has been taken so far.*

I quote Recommendation 17 in full:

> *"We recommend finally that in all future policy decisions touching and concerning Mining of all types in Sierra Leone, it must always be borne in mind and must always be reflected in all concessions, contracts, leases, and licenses granted to ANY PERSON to mine in Sierra Leone, that the precious mineral being mined, be it diamonds, gold or any other,*

> *BELONGS EXCLUSIVELY to the people of Sierra Leone present and future, and that the People of Sierra Leone are entitled to benefit from their God-given natural resource as much as possible instead of being handed a pittance from the minerals mined here, with the Investor carting off the Lion's Share every time. There is need for a radical change of Policy in this regard."*

It is also well known and internationally acknowledged that Sierra Leone possesses substantial marine resources, which is why every night hundreds if not thousands of Poachers enter our territorial waters to steal our fish, shrimps, etc with no-one to stop them. Boats come here from as far afield as Russia, China, Korea, etc. to plunder our continental shelf and go away, while there is hardly any fish in the local markets for our people to eat. It is a well-known fact that those who are supposed to monitor such activities are often in the pay of the trespassers and criminals who even have the audacity to come here with factory-ships all of which operate to our detriment.

After 50 years of Independence, is it not time we take full charge of our resources and make sure our people benefit from them? Are we not tired of begging?

It is my submission Ladies and Gentlemen, that after 50 Years of Independence it is time for us to assert ourselves as a Nation, it is time for us to rely on ourselves and to stop crying down ourselves and our compatriots and to rely on Foreigners for everything. Every day you hear the Sierra Leone Ruling Class praying for and calling for "INVESTORS".—Investors are not Philanthropists but Businessmen, and they come here to make a profit for themselves and their Shareholders, not to help us solve our problems. There are a lot of things we can do for ourselves for which we do not need to rely on Investors, and it is my plea to all Sierra Leoneans on this day that we need to be self-reliant as far as possible.

We need to believe in ourselves and to stop thinking that Foreigners can do everything better than we can.

Let me now look briefly at a few other areas where in my view we have not helped ourselves much over the years.

Medical Facilities: It is a well known fact that medical facilities in Sierra Leone leave much to be desired. I speak from personal experience as I had to rush out of the Country in January last year on the advice of my doctor for a procedure which is really quite a simple one but which was not available here, and as a direct consequence of that procedure I had to undergo a major operation immediately, and may have died if I had not been in a position to go to Britain.

After 50 years of Independence ought we not to have proper medical facilities in our Country? Nowadays you hear every other person with a medical problem going to GHANA for treatment. Ghana achieved Independence only 4 years before we did, but they have now left us far behind. With the very small population we have, coupled with the vast natural resources at our disposal, ought we not to be in a position to provide proper medical facilities in our Country? Quite recently, I know of someone who was rushed to the Connaught Hospital in the middle of the night, but there was not a single doctor available, and he had to be taken to a private doctor in his home for which service he had to pay quite a substantial sum of money. But what if he could not afford it? As we all know His Excellency The President launched Free Medical Care for Pregnant and Lactating Mothers and Children under 5 years—

A most laudable venture indeed! But what is happening on the ground? Most of the time the medicines are not available and the women have to buy them outside the hospitals, which in my view defeats the intention of the Scheme.

That takes me back to the Shakespearian quotation that

> **"the fault is in ourselves, and not in our Stars."**

There are many other areas I would have liked to touch on, but I think I will leave those for the discussion,—such as Education, the serious deterioration of standards in the Schools and Universities; the non-improvement of the Airport as compared to Banjul International, or Kotoka International, Accra, and Abidjan Airport; rampant corruption, and the lack of electricity and water supply in many parts of the Country not least in the Capital City, Freetown.

At Independence we had a functioning Railway from Water Street, Freetown to as far as Pendembu in Kailahun. Those among us who are old enough will remember that there was a railway track along the Street now known as 'OLD RAILWAY LINE, TENGBEH TOWN" leading upto Hill Station, where the Expatriate members of the Colonial Establishment used to live. What happened our Railway? It was phased out, for reasons which are not clear to me, thereby depriving ourselves of an excellent opportunity of transportation of People and Goods, especially produce from the Provinces to Freetown which has not been replaced. Another missed opportunity? Another misplaced priority?

When I started practice in 1974 there was Sierra Leone Airways which used to fly from Hastings Airfield to Bo, Kenema, Yengema and Bonthe. There was also the direct flight from Freetown to London and back, with Sierra Leonean Air Hostesses on board the Planes. What happened to all of that? Now there is absolutely no internal flight within Sierra Leone. At present People as well as Goods have to be moved by road ONLY, there is no transport by rail or by air. Another missed opportunity? Another misplaced priority? Far from making progress, have we not retrogressed and gone backwards?

There was a time when Fourah Bay College known as "The Athens of West Africa". Classical Scholars among us will know that the name "Athens" signified the origin of knowledge, wisdom and enlightenment, which in turn tells you the kind of respect which was accorded to our Country at that time as it was not only the Headquarters of the Colonial Establishment in West Africa, but even after Independence Sierra Leone in the form of Fourah Bay College used to be a magnet to which Students from other West African Countries were attracted.

As a student at Fourah Bay college [which was then affiliated to The University of Durham,] from 1965 to 1969, under

the enlightened leadership and direction of distinguished Scholars like Dr. Davidson Nicol; Prof. The Rev. Canon Henry Sawyerr; and my own Professor Dr. Eldred Jones, I know the very high standard of Education and Discipline that we enjoyed at Fourah Bay College, not to mention the available facilities like Constant Electricity and Water supply; three(3) Square Meals a day; a well-stocked Library, and the list goes on.

What happened to all of that? I need not tell you what is happening today because you all know. Poor Standard of Education, Examination malpractices, Cultism and violence on campus, etc. etc. Once again, what is happening to our "Athens"?

Another missed opportunity?

In Conclusion, Mr. Chairman, Ladies and Gentlemen, my final message to all my compatriots on this Golden Jubilee of our Independence is as follows:

After 50 years of Independence, it is time for us to wake up out of our national slumber; It is time for us to pull ourselves up by our bootstraps;

It is time for us to be self-reliant, to know what is good for us and to stop relying on Foreigners for everything; It is time for us to treat each other with respect, and to applaud the efforts of others and not to cry them down even when they are trying hard; It is time for us to ensure that we harness our natural resources to our full benefit and to stop allowing "So-called Investors" to take away our God-given wealth giving back to us only a pittance; It is time for us and for the Ruling Class especially to love our Country more than our pockets;

> *It is time for Sierra Leone to take her place in the top half of the Human Development Index, alongside Countries like Malaysia and Singapore with whom we were once at par; It is time for us to stop being a "wretchedly poor Country", and to stop BEGGING all the time; It is time for Sierra Leone and all Sierra Leoneans to work with sincerity and commitment for ourselves and for our children and grandchildren yet unborn. **And it is time for us to stop attempting to reap where we have not sown.***
>
> ***HEARTY CONGRATULATIONS to all Sierra Leoneans on this our Golden Jubilee of our Independence, and may our eyes be truly open from this day forward!***
>
> ***LONG LIVE SIERRA LEONE! May God Bless all Sierra Leoneans! Thank you for your kind attention."***

Until when utilitarian thinkers modified their behaviour through the introduction of 'rule' utilitarianism, which prevented the practice from looking at every act in isolation, as in the case of 'act' utilitarianism, <u>the introduction of moral rules was meant for assessing utility for everyone in society.</u> Therefore on these moral grounds, it has been argued and established that acts like murder, stealing, lying, thuggery and so on were outlawed to give way to position moral values in civilized societies as put forward by T. Tamsjo (2002).

Contractualist Ethics was the work of the seventeenth century thinker Thomas Hobbes (1588-1679) which focused on making distinctions between ethical rights and wrongs. If the whole world in which human beings exist is known to be one country called the "state of nature", without any form of political, social and legal authorities and organisations, Hobbes argues that there will be no meaningful justification between just and unjust, right and wrong, good and bad and everybody will be doing whatever they want, whenever they want and wherever they want, regardless of how silly and unethical their actions may be.

However, individual humans all possess self contained machines driven by negative (fear) and positive (desire) energy, but with the capacity for instrumental reason, so that they can calculate how to attain or avoid outcomes.

As the fear of death and the concomitant desire for self preservation is fundamental across all human beings, Hobbesian individuals, when placed in the 'state of nature', Hobbes argues that there will be a condition of war of 'all against all', not necessarily because humans are nasty and evil against each other, but without any guarantee of security, they are forced by their overwhelming fear of death and desire for self preservation to accumulate as much power to themselves as possible to prevent eventual attack from others as possible, a kind of jungle justice where only the fittest survives.

The life of Hobbesians, living in the 'state of nature' are 'solitary, poor, nasty, brutish and short' in particular because peoples fundamental desire; the desire to live is very often abused because of the entire absence of trust between human beings in their natural state, which can't just let them decide to stop killing each other. As it happened in Sierra Leone during the ten years civil conflict when the 'Kamajors', the civil defense forces grouped themselves to defend their communities against attacks from both rebel and government military forces, (government soldiers who became known as 'sobels—soldiers in the day and rebels at night'). This situation continued until the Lome Peace Accord in Togo on 25 May 1999 and 7 July 1999 under the auspices of the chairman of the Economic Community of West African States (ECOWAS), President, Gnassingbe Eyadema, president of Togo, another West

African state not too close to Sierra Leone (www.sierraleone.org. lomeaccord.yuiik8uol9html).

This meeting set the agreement that covenanted and socially contracted the fighting forces to drop arms for peace. The 'Theory of Justice', according to Rawl (1971), what were arrived at during this summit were all those factors put together (general things about human nature and behavior, history, social institutions, different ways of organizing political communities, and so on) to formulate the contract which became 'the veil of ignorance' that bonded all the warring parties in the name of peace, basically in their own interest.

Rawl's contractualism on this occasion practically echoes that of earlier examples of the social contract tradition; that fundamental rights of every human cannot be traded off for the benefits of others.

No innocent person can be sacrificed to save the life of others, even if he or she volunteers to do so, with the exception of Christian believers in the case of Jesus Christ, Holy Bible (New International Version John, Chapter 1: 29, 12:23, 14:1-4 and 19:1-41 (1984, International Bible Society in Canada and USA).

Contractualism, however, is set to making distinctions between those people with whom one is in contractual community and those who are outside the contract. The Lome Peace Accord, for example, of 25 May 1999 and 7 July 1999 therefore became respected contractual agreement in Sierra Leone, binding all warring factions together, as put by (Freeman, 2006) and (Pettit, 2006). These and other factors make contractualism, a foundational requirements assumption about human individuals.

Other rationalist ethical theorists including: the Deontological theory whose first approach focused on moral theory such as the rule based approach to ethics concluding that moral principles have an absolute and categorical perspective status. The moral claim of divine rights is practically unquestionable.

The knowledge of moral truths according to the Christian tradition in medieval times was understood to be available through the scriptures, although available through natural reasons. This natural law understanding, Kant, (1981 [1785]) helped greatly in calculating what was good and was bad; what was beautiful and what was ugly. To do the right thing for the wrong reason is not moral, according to Kant's moral principles.

One must work out first what is the right thing to do-meaning the identification of the requirements of the universal moral law, and second to act on that basis rather than taking decisions based on individual desires of fulfillment and satisfaction.

The Kantian ethics attracted attention of Hill (2006) and O'Neill (1993) that resulted into the "universalisation test: *Always lie to protect ones feelings" for example, was universally unaccepted and immoral.* By enslaving a human being is violation of what makes humanity special and reduces not the enslaved but rather the enslaver to the condition of an animal incapable of respecting the self determined moral law as Alex Haley (2007) puts it in Roots.

When a person capable of knowing the moral law, acts in violation of it, then he or she is found guilty of immorality and should be held responsible for what he or she has done. *Those who profited in slavery like the Barclays family in Britain will ever remain in the history of Africa as being immoral and evil.*

However, William Wilberforce (24 August 1759-29 July 1833), a British politician who was also an evangelical Christian started the slave trade abolition movement, through the persuasion of Thomas Clarkson and group of slave trade activists including Granville Sharp, Hannah More and Charles Middleton until the Slave Trade Act in 1807. (www. wikipedia.org/william_wilberforce). Deontological ethics endows all human beings with an absolute moral status.

This has significance implications for thinking about killing and punishment within Global Ethics.

Among the Discourse Ethics in which, the Herberman's moral theory formalised the universalisation of certain morals, such as drug trades, slavery and torture of human beings in certain cultures or misappropriation of public funds by top officers (government ministers, permanent secretaries and high civil servants) in certain governments, as morally wrong, no matter where life exist, goes beyond the borders to provoke the debate under fair conditions of argumentation between citizens of rich states and citizens of poor states about the justifiability of current global economic inequality. Would such an argument necessarily result in an agreement to redistribute wealth from the rich to the poor?

Are the rich states justified to introduce strict border control measures to prevent economic migrants from countries they have once colonised and "exploited"; they now referred to as poor nations. Where lies the morale of western powers who once established colonies in poorer nations to turn their backs away on these nations and even consider them uncivilised?

Would the moral justification be embedded in assisting those poor nations to develop their resources through education and skill trainings for the citizens to be sufficient enough in their countries so that they are discouraged into economic migration? Could one of these be the availability of Educational Qualifications (both academic and professional) at affordable prices in former colonies so that the citizens stay there to study and qualify from their "colonial masters" countries without degrading into economic migrants? Would the local educational development be strengthen to be self sufficient enough to match in ranks and standard with those foreign ones they still value and consider as yard sticks of measurements?

Sierra Leone, for example, equates their qualifications to British standard because of first, their British colonial linkage and secondly because of the formal affiliation of their first college of higher learning (Fourah Bay College) with the Durham University, a major higher learning institution in Britain from 1876 till January 1965, when the University of Sierra Leone was formerly instituted through a Royal Charter (www.Expadica.com/uk/education/higher).

Industrial relations problems in British schools always emerge from different angles and solutions therefore varies. Seifert (1991a) looked at the sources of most of these problems as lack of strategic management at the earlier stage of the recent education reforms and came out with three solutions to the problem:

Firstly, he suggested the "liberal pluralist" solution; i.e. the reformulation and reinstatement of the post war trade union movement to be held responsible for central negotiation purposes which also favoured by the major teachers union (the NUT and NASUWT) and even LEA managers and some political heavy weights within the Labour party. Secondly, to apply a managerial system within the resource management initiatives where responsibilities are traced to reduce the role of trade unions at the LEA stage and thirdly, the introduction of radical practices to coincide with radical changes.

Institutional development leads to improvements in the standard of education and improvement of examination results to attract more students so that the resources gained are used to recruit and retain quality staff. Purchase of school system materials are geared towards the staff and student support systems in schools. Bach and Winchester (1994) picked some of the problems related to pay scale rated between males and females in the British education systems which they recommended changes to facilitate more decentralised system within.

THE PEACE-DEAL ELECTION AND TRANSFER OF POWER FOR PEACE MAINTENANCE

The three stages of conflict resolution for a peace deal:

What is a conflict?

A conflict is a dispute that occurs between two parties emanating from misunderstanding or disagreement over an issue or a deal. This situation is usually common and it happens between couples (husband and wife), brothers and sisters of the same family, in government, different political parties, etc. As conflict is therefore a feeling that results into accusing one party by the other party, of inflicting what they do not like or being treated unfairly, against the law, the dispute might result into quarrelling, fighting, tribalism, racism, segregation, civil war, international war, etc. Once a conflict start, it develops to different stages and the consequence could be devastating costing fines, properties or even lives that may include the innocent, the poor, the rich, women, children, and the powerful in high places. We have all witnessed conflict and the result unfolded in Libya which resulted into costing "the head of state" his life, including some members of his family and many other citizens. My personal advice to my readers is that: "don't encourage conflict to start and carry on in any relationship".

Of course, Sierra Leoneans have once experienced conflicts (arm conflict) perpetrated by Foday Sankoh and his Revolutionary United Front (RUF). According to Foday Sankoh, he was not pleased the mannerism in which Siaka Stevens and the All Peoples Congress (APC) mismanaged the wealth of Sierra Leone and for many years he went on studying and developing strategies to bring the situation to the attention of the nation and his research discovered that the only way that everybody was to take him serious was through rebel-group formation to put across their demand on behalf of the country that would halt APC as a ruling force. Although Siaka Stevens was already dead by then, Joseph Siadu Momoh, who was his predecessor, the APC leader and head of state of Sierra Leone cowered and flew into neighbouring Guinea, when junior army officers from the civil war front, arrived at state house to solicit for funding to buy foods and medicines and this motivated the junta regime headed by young Valentine E M Strasser.

First stage of conflict resolution: Once a conflict start, it develops to different stages and the devastating effects could be catastrophic resulting into divorce as far as wars, etc. My personal advice to my readers, as I said earlier on, is that: "don't encourage conflict to start and carry on in any relationship".

Although this is sometimes unavoidable in our relationship, especially when one party feels advantaged of the disadvantage suffered by the other.

The first step to conflict resolution is to **accept that there is an unacceptable condition** and it should be straightened for the benefits of all. Accept your own part of the blame and take every responsibility genuinely.

Second stage-Peace process: At this stage, all parties will be ready to negotiate to enhance the conflict resolution. This stage is the most painful because during this time, all parties are required to give up most of what they valued as being precious to satisfy the other party in order that both remain happy and live together without disturbance from any party, ever after. What they give up most is the peace deal.

The third stage-Peace maintenance: This stage is usually the most fragile of the conflict resolution process. At this stage, the parties involved in the peace process and affected by the conflict will reflect on how well they acted and what benefits they got from the resolution or peace process. It is therefore fragile because any party can feel that they have been tricked and led into agreeing into signing a deal that is not in their own interest and that the deal is not fair on them. Such pressures may cause the negotiation leaders to break the peace deal and start the conflict all over again. The peace deal therefore continues during the peace maintenance period in order to hold the peace. How was this handled in Sierra Leone peace process and what were the peace deal?

Tajan Kabbah's role:

Whether anybody likes it or not, SLPP's Tejan Kabbah is the most strategic president Sierra Leone has ever got in the history of politics of that country. He assumed presidential power to perform the most important task the country ever needed at the right time, for the right purpose; in the middle of civil war, when there as no time for him to enjoy presidential "sweet of office" and subsequently further, his wife fell ill of cancer and died as a result.

When that wound was just very fresh in the minds of the state, it was the time when the All Peoples Congress (APC) supporters went into their jubilation of singing in the streets of Freetown with their new invention of provocation "Tejan Kabbah na Koboko" meaning that Tejan Kabbah has no wife. May I take this moment, in my capacity as a genuine Sierra Leonean, to please apologise to Tejan Kabbah and express my personal disgust for such a shameful display of unacceptable behaviour, because that is not Sierra Leonean in any capacity, where-ever. Tejan Kabbah's term of office will ever be remembered as the term of "peace search era" in Sierra Leone.

He embarked immediately on peace search mission by visiting Foday Sankoh and the RUF in the bush to discuss how best they can come to terms leading to cessation of conflict in the country, ass he accepted that there was a problem.

I came to learn the practical theory from Sierra Leone experience that peace negotiation in theory, always requires giving up some benefits to your opponent and sometimes the peace deal cost very dearly but beneficial as long as the peace deal comes to fruition. Also, a peace deal, as in Sierra Leone's case starts with such sacrifices, and continues during and **after the peace negotiation, to maintain the peace process**. Tejan Kabbah had to come to terms with Foday Sankoh to the extent of appointing that rebel leader as the vice president of Sierra Leone in charge of all mineral resources in the country including diamonds, the nation's source of wealth.

As a result, some very strong SLPP party supporters who did not understand the strategy found Tejan Kabbah disgusting, unacceptable and difficult to work with; fell out with him and eventually left the party and some even switched over to other parties while others started their own political party and collided with other parties to undermine SLPP strongholds.

Another major problem Tejan Kabbah had with SLPP supporters was that he was never frequent in the party office, but his excuse was that he was not a president for SLPP but a president of Sierra Leone, the nation and therefore his office of frequency was the state house office, where he deals with state affairs.

Therefore, the APC's victory of 2007 that took Ernest Koroma to state house was still part of the peace deal agreement (**peace maintenance-after peace deal**) of Sierra Leone negotiated by Tejan Kabbah; although to great shock of Solomon Berewa with the APC as the they have raised high level of threats for starting the war all over again because the RUF overthrew their democratically elected government for which Joseph Saidu Momoh was the leader.

That has worked well for the country and thank God for bringing strategic Tejan Kabbah at that crucial time and to use him well for the benefits of all in Sierra Leone.

The 2012 presidential election is watched carefully as the real test-case of political genuine and leadership of the country and we remain to pray that it will go on without another phase of civil war because we are just very tired and would like to get on with our lives as politicians are not the only human beings living in Sierra Leone in as much as they are very highly respected.

BIBLIOGRAPHY

1. Bardwell and Holden (1997), Human Resources Management, A contemporary perspective, Second Edition. Pitman publishing

2. Bach, S and Winchester, D (2003) 'Industrial elations in the public sector' in P. Edwards (ed.) <u>Industrial Relations</u>, Blackwell: Oxford

3. Bentham, J. (1982 [1789]). An Introduction to the Principles of Morals and Legislation, ed. J. H. Burns and H. I. A. Hart, London:Methuen.

4. Freeman, S. (2006) 'Morality Contractarianism as a Foundation for Interpersonal Morality', in Drier (ed), Contemporary Debates, <u>pp. 55-75.</u>

5. Haley, A. (May 2007), Roots Perfection Learning (USA)

6. Hill, T. E. (2006) 'Kantian Normative Ethics', in Copp (ed.), <u>Oxford Handbook pp. 480-541.</u>

7. Hobbes, T. (1991 [1651]) Leviathan, ed. R. Tuck, Cambridge: Cambridge University Press

8. Hutchings, K. (2010) Global Ethics, Polity Press

9. Kant, I. (1981 [1785]) Grounding for Metaphysics of Morals, trants. J. W. Ellington, Indianapolis: Hacket

10. Mill, J. S., (1962 [1961]) *Utilitilitariansm,* ed. M. Warnock, London, Fontana

11. O'Neil (1993) 'Kanitian Ethics', in Singer (ed.), A Comparion, <u>pp. 175-85.</u>

12. Petit, P. (1993) 'Consequentialisms' in Singer (ed.), <u>A Companion, pp230-48.</u> An introductory overview of ethical consequentialism, including utilitarianism.

13. Petit, P. (2006) 'Can Contract Theory Ground Morality?' in Dreier (ed.), <u>Contemporary Debates pp. 76-96.</u>

14. Seifert, R. (1991a) "The conflict potential pages" <u>pages41-43, from Managing Schools Today</u>

15. Shaw, W. (2006) 'The Consequentialist Persepective', in Dreier (ed), Contemporary Debates, pp5-20. A defence of ethical consequentialism.

16. Tamsjo, T. (2002) Understanding Ethics: An Introduction to Mral Theory, Edinburgh, Edinburgh University Press

17. <u>www.kopcourses</u> <u>Human Resources.</u> Marcels De Resende at the Kaplan Open Learning of Essex University in UK.

18. <u>www.wikipedia.org</u>

19. <u>www.sierraleone.org/lomeaccord</u>

20. <u>www.wikipedia.org/williamwilberforce</u>

21. www.expadica.com/wk/education/higher

www.ingramcontent.com/pod-product-compliance
Lightning Source LLC
Chambersburg PA
CBHW061250280526
45784CB00002B/706